"Years after our first encounter at Family Court, a chance meeting brought us together a second time at a local deli counter. The story Michael shared about our first meeting, one I didn't remember, was filled with such depth and emotion about his life and circumstances, both of us were brought to tears in the middle of the store. I hesitantly accepted the invitation to visit his restaurant, which is the last and only hesitation I have had in our relationship. Michael has shown honestly and integrity in his personal and professional life. He works endlessly to make his dreams and goals a reality. Michael has faced obstacles, but with the grace of God, he is able to show compassion, humility and a strong ethical character. Michael has a gregarious personality, enjoys joking, exaggerating and being the life of the party. He is a true entertainer with a dynamic voice. Michael has the encouragement of his partner Laura, a dynamo in her own right. Together they have put together a wonderful restaurant, an amazing band and a place to make pleasurable memories, reminiscent of old Las Vegas. Michael and Laura have become steadfast friends. I hope that all the effort Michael has put into writing his novel, will allow the truth of his life to be heard. His hard work is inspiring and I wish him the best of luck in all his future endeavors."

Steve Rushfield

"Chef Mike is an amazing man—supremely talented on stage and in the kitchen, boundless energy and an unbelievable big heart. That he still has these qualities after all he has been through, is testimony to his character and spirit. He is truly one of a kind!"

Hal Holzman

DECEIT
CORRUPTION
COVER-UP

Michael Leonetti

Deceit Corruption Cover-up
All Rights Reserved
Copyright © 2019 by Michael Leonetti

This book may not be reproduced or transmitted in whole or in part, in any form or by any means electronic or mechanical, including photocopying, scanning, recording, or any information storage or retrieval system, without prior permission in writing from the authors.

Printed in the United States of America
First Printing 2019

Book design by www.delaney-designs.com

ISBN: 978-0-57861-951-4

This book is dedicated to those who
truly stuck by my side because
to love is to feel.

THE STORY OF MICHAEL LEONETTI

This book was written and documented to show how corrupt and dishonest a government could be to cover up not only the truth but to hide the inequities of justice in our judicial system. But most of all this story is told to show there is a God and a Higher Power.

Chapter 1

LIFE IN PHILADELPHIA

In the 1950's Italian South Philadelphia was a pretty great place to grow up. With rows upon rows of brownstones, closely knit neighbors were a natural part of life. Each watching the other, kids and parents felt safe and secure. No one had to go far to obtain anything needed, it was all supplied within a short walking distance. There was the local butcher, a grocery store, a beauty shop, a bakery, a cheese shop, a clothing boutique, an appliance store, two churches, an elementary and high school and a smattering of bars and restaurants. Their entire world revolved between 9th Street and Broad Street. What the Leonetti household supplied to the cloistered Italian neighborhood was the essential undertaking service and his grandfather's flower shop embellished the funeral. When the weekends rolled around, Michael, as a preschooler, spent all his time with his grandparents who owned the brownstone ten paces away. To say the family was close knit was an understatement as they all lived on the same block in identical homes built at the turn of the 1900's.

MICHAEL LEONETTI

Grandpa Michael's face held a perpetual smile when in the presence of his namesake grandson. Showering the toddler with hugs, kisses and constant attention, he relished every moment before walking down two flights to the basement and assembling magnificent floral arrangements;

Life in the brownstones was filled with love, activity, work and a constant juggling of space. Initially, after Dolores' (Michael's mom) divorce, she returned to her parent's home with her infant. Three generations lived within the tight interior of the three-story brownstone. Four cement steps led to the first-floor florist shop, the place where Grandfather Michael made his livelihood but it was in the basement where he cobbled together the exquisite floral designs which were sought after by brides, widows and widowers. And this was the location of the sacred second bathroom where he never had to wait his turn.

On the first floor, in back of the small store front, a narrow hallway led to the kitchen measuring seven by four feet, a living room, measuring ten by ten, and a dining room that could miraculously seat twenty people. One can only surmise that no one in the Leonetti family had an extra pound of flesh on their body or they wouldn't fit around the dining table. (Which was not the case for most of their neighbors).

An oak staircase trailed up two more flights. The second floor held two bedrooms and one tile bathroom fitted with both a shower and bathtub which was shared between three adults and one young toddler. Luxurious bubble baths were usually out of the question unless someone picked a rare moment when everyone was out of the house. Michael made it easy on his family, opting for a shower, which was quick and simple. "The shower had five heads. When I stood in the stall my whole body had warm water at the same time. It felt great." That was as far as Michael ventured in the house because his grandpa had rented the two bedrooms on the third floor to two friends. Each paid fifteen dollars a month for the privilege of living in individual rooms, in the center of the safest neighborhood in Philadelphia. The two men took advantage of the situation and remained in those two bedrooms for thirty-five years paying the same fifteen dollars. Grandpa Michael was a man of his word, virtue spilling from every pore in his body and soul. His word was as good as gold. For all the years young Michael grew up he was banished from the top floor.

"Those men paid for their privacy," reminded Grandpa.

They kept to themselves, never partook in the family meals and paid the rent the first of each month. On Saturday mornings, Grandpa Michael prepared the floral arrangements for the evening weddings. Back then, the florist and his wife were always invited to the wedding as guests. Almost every Saturday night, Julie and Michael dressed for a wedding. She wore an elegant gown and Michael wore church attire, a white shirt, a striped tie, a navy suit. As young as three, they dressed their grandson identically to his grandpa and brought him along. Michael was always well-behaved and when he was four, the band allowed him a chance to play one song on the drums. That was the beginning of his performing career. He already had a passion for music, but when the crowd stood and cheered the preschooler, the love of entertaining was instilled in his heart. Nothing ever gave him as much pleasure or happiness as when he was in front of a group of people pounding out beats on the drums. At the age of four he knew exactly what he wanted to do, and never altered that dream.

Chapter 2

Sunday was the most important day of the week, the day the Leonetti family gave thanks to the Lord for all His blessings. It didn't matter if snow was falling, or pellets of rain bounced off their raincoats, or if bitter northern winds whipped their hats off their heads, the family trudged to St. Nicholas. The quintessential community Catholic church, each Sunday it was guaranteed every pew would be filled and when the silver bowl was passed around, it was returned brimming over with cash. If the saints had been especially generous to a parishioner, that would translate into more money in the offering bowl. When a church goer hit the lucky number, or there was a new birth, or a special anniversary, the blessed church goer always thanked the Lord (or the saint) with an extra donation at the morning service. It costs a lot of money to maintain the church, its clergy and the services it provided to the community. Whenever possible a little extra cash was always welcome. Michael was dressed like his grandfather, two generations of white cotton shirts, navy striped ties and navy suits as they paraded into the main sanctuary. Dolores and Julie were dressed in simple woolen dresses and low heels, no perfume, no jewelry and little make-up. They were humbled in the presence of their Lord and vanity was frowned upon. Stepmother and daughter made sure the men properly crossed themselves, pointed to an empty pew and the family sat in silence as they waited for the clergy to appear.

Even though it was difficult to keep Michael completely attentive during the service, his eyes wandered around, he was kept busy gawking at the majesty inside the cathedral. The way the sunlight streamed through the stained glass, the outstretched arms of the saints above the alter, the vestments of the priest, the albs of the altar boys, the silver chalice for wine, the ciborium for the Host, and the oil paintings covering the walls. For this young child the colors, textures, sounds and smells of the Catholic service, kept his mind occupied and his legs and arms still. Two hours later, the family emerged from the Church, thanked the priest and walked home. Dolores always said a silent prayer thanking God for keeping her busy son quiet. Two hours was a long time for anyone to sit, especially an active child. The wooden pews furnished with thin red velvet cushions did little to add comfort to the congregation and especially an active child.

Walking home every member of the family was mentally planning the balance of their day. For Grandpa Michael, it was reading the Philadelphia Inquirer from front to back, for Dolores it was setting the table, and polishing silverware, for Julie it was preparing a meal for twenty. The cast of characters was always the same as was the menu, yet everyone was happy and loved the predictability. Tradition, that was the one ingredient that held the family together. They never tired of conversing with the same people, eating the same meal, it was their family tradition and it would remain so until, well no one had the answer to that.

Frank (Julie's brother) was always the first to arrive. Carrying a large bottle of red wine, he prodigiously handed it to Grandpa Michael, and held the front door open for his wife, Christina, who was followed by five active and hungry children. That alone would burst the seams of most living rooms. Moments later, around two-fifteen in the afternoon, Johnny, (Dolores' brother-in-law) was also carrying a large bottle of red wine. He also held the door open for his wife Carmela, followed by their three hungry children. To say the brownstone was a frenzy of activity was an understatement.

Dolores always knew exactly how many chairs and place settings were required at the dining table. She was cognizant she had the easy chores as her stepmother toiled away in a kitchen which was barely larger than a linen closet. Magic that was how Grandpa Michael described the Sunday meal which emerged from the kitchen.

Once everyone was seated, Louis opened two bottles of wine and poured generous portions into the glasses. Julie's first course was a huge ceramic platter filled with cold antipasto; roasted peppers, olives of every color and size, cheeses, anchovies and thinly cured salami and prosciutto. Dolores tore off hunks of homemade Italian bread and passed it around the table with virgin olive oil. No one was in a hurry, they had the entire afternoon to graze. Lively conversation was always guaranteed. Armed with the knowledge of the Sunday newspaper, the men discussed business, politics and whatever covered the front page while the mothers discussed child rearing, fashion, make-up, recipes and of course their kids. The second course was homemade cheese raviolis smothered in marinara sauce. Each ravioli was perfectly square and melted in the mouth.

In the winter months, young Michael remarked how he could see steam rising in the air above the serving bowl set in the middle of the table. Empty dishes were quickly passed to Dolores as she ladled portions into the hand painted porcelain dishes. The plate design quickly disappeared under a mound of red sauce and oozing pale ricotta cheese. The empty serving bowl was brought back to the kitchen and returned to the table piled high with meatballs smothered in the same red sauce. The recipe was a well-guarded secret handed down from generation to generation. Julie would pick the right time to pass that on to her step-daughter but not today, Dolores wasn't ready. Decades later Michael would write a cookbook unveiling his Grandma's recipes but those meatballs, those delectable morsels of ground meat, would NEVER be revealed. Some things were so sacred they were carried to the grave and so it would stand with Leonetti meatball recipe.

Louis (Michael's stepfather) kept the wine and water glasses replenished and constantly begged Julie to sit a while and enjoy the company. Her answer was always the same, "I'll be fine, I'll eat later. We have to take of our guests."

He always predicted her response but felt compelled to

let her know she was appreciated and needed.

"The next course needs my attention. Sausages can be tricky and I have another loaf of bread to take out of the oven," Julie added. Just when their stomachs were stuffed and there was hardly room for another bite, Julie filled a platter with steak braciola and another with chicken Neapolitan, both family secrets. Louis grabbed the heavy dishes and set them in the center of the table and Dolores placed portions on everyone's plates.

Walking out of the narrow kitchen, Julie wiped her sweaty forehead and finally took a seat at the table. Louis handed her a glass of wine, kissed her on the cheek and announced, "Ma, you did it again. You made the best meal in the Italian neighborhood."

Everyone raised their glasses and toasted the cook. Seated amongst the women, she had plenty to add to the conversation but it would never be her recipes.

"Johnny always says to me, why can't you cook like Julie?" wined Carmela.

"I look at him and remind him that you have all these secrets and that's why I can't cook like you. It's like you are some kind of an artist when it comes to cooking. You paint with sauces and the meats are your canvass. So, I look him straight in the eye and tell him how lucky we are to be related to you and to enjoy this weekly meal. That shuts him up until around Wednesday evening when I usually burn the chicken breasts."

The women had a good laugh, continued sipping on the wine and eventually passed the empty plates to the end of the table and Julie carted them into the kitchen. Coffee and dessert would be served after the dishes had been washed and everyone had a chance to digest the heavy meal.

Because there were twenty guests it was almost always someone's birthday. After the last loaf of bread was extracted from the oven, Julie would pop in three cake pans, enough for a huge triple tiered cake. It was always a vanilla buttercream batter but the frostings varied with the occasion. Sometimes the frosting was chocolate, or lemon, or orange and sometimes it was laced with Amaretto. A few candles dotted the top of the cake, candles were blown out and it was dissected into twenty portions. In the colder months Julie served coffee but in the heat of the summer, she added ice to pitchers of water and ice-tea.

After the last cake crumb was devoured, the children dispersed to the street and played ball. It was a unique game which required a half ball and a broom stick. The ball would be pitched to a kid standing across the street and points were awarded based upon where the ball landed. There was the first-floor window, second-floor window and if the ball went over the roof it was a home run! The true point of the game was to stay alive as the cars swished by. Luckily, no one had to deal with such a tragedy. It was Sunday and the Italians understood tradition, driving their cars with care.

At seven o'clock, the mothers gathered their children, thanked Julie, kissed each other (which took at least ten minutes) and walked to their perspective homes. Everyone had a smile, a story to tell, an ache or a pain to share, but the most important memory each would carry away from the afternoon, was the love of family. Surrounded by a cluster of people who really cared for each other, they felt secure, and confident they could get through anything life would hand out. True, they had the church, but the weekly touch, the kiss, the handshake, the patient understanding of a cousin, aunt or uncle, made their lives richer and meaningful.

Chapter 3

FOR THE LOVE OF MUSIC

It seemed implausible that anything could supersede the importance of the pungent smell of freshly chopped garlic simmering in a deep cast iron pot waiting for the next pound of freshly ground meat from the local butcher to be married together.

Yet above and beyond young Michael's love and passion for Italian food came his love and passion for music. How could a four-year old pick up a pair of makeshift drum sticks and create music? It was in the basement where Grandpa Michael nurtured Michael's love and god given talent for music. There was always music playing while the florist worked on his craft and when the metal cans that were once filled with fresh flowers had been emptied, he would turn them upside down and create a drum set for his grandson. Using the long rods that molded the intricate floral designs, he would cut them down and make drum sticks and the two of them would beat the drums for hours to the latest tunes on the radio. The low ceiling kept the noise to a minimum and no one complained about the banging. Grandpa Michael played the radio but had an extensive collection of records. He collected modern crooners, and jazz performers, the best sounds in music, and encouraged his grandson to play along to the tunes. Tommy Dorsey, Louis Prima, and Frank Sinatra were his favorites but when Gene Krupa, a spectacular drummer, was pounding in the background, little Michael grabbed his sticks and emulated the very same beats. Both Grandpa and grandson had a passion for music and a talent for playing drums but it would be the grandson who saw his musical aspirations become reality.

When Saturday night weddings rolled around and the grandparents arrived with their grandson, it was the grandson who became the hit of the wedding.

One evening, the band was playing many of the same tunes that were spinning in Grandpa Michael's basement and the preschooler knew every note and every beat. During the break Grandpa Michael asked the band leader if his grandson could sit in on just one song.

They looked down at the small child, laughed and said, "Why not?" When the band returned Michael took the seat at the set of drums and he played like a professional.

Many of the guests turned to watch the four-year-old. When the song was over they applauded and Michael stood up and bowed. That was the beginning of Michael's career in the music business.

Grandpa's eyes were riveted to his grandson while he was on the stage, the child's smile his enthusiasm and the genuine feel for the music was evident. On the walk home,

Grandpa made a decision, he would buy his grandson a real set of drums. He was saving money and couldn't think of a better way to invest it other than for his grandson's future. It was as if he were destined to play the drums. A few days later Grandpa called Michael to the basement and pointed to a set of drums, "These are for you," he said. Michael was over whelmed with joy.

He hugged his grandpa, grabbed the drumsticks and never put them down. Crashing and banging was heard for hours on end and there was one wide smile attached to every beat. At four, this young child had found his destiny.

What seemed to be a tight house was now a little roomier. When Dolores remarried and moved out there was an empty bedroom. It was time to give little grandson Michael his own space.

Julie redecorated the space and her grandson finally slept in a real bed instead of a cot. But the household was never quiet. Between the blasting drums in the basement, music spinning nonstop, customers floating in and out of the florist storefront at all hours of the day, and the constant banging of pots and pans, the home was teeming with life.

Two doors down, with the arrival of a new baby, Dolores and Louis' household was also teeming with life; Joy, was a healthy perfect baby who was loved and cared for by an extended family.

As Michael grew older, and his drum playing more in demand, it was he who became the star of the wedding.

Grandpa Michael proudly escorted their grandson to every event and sat with a boastful look as guests danced to the music and the beat of the drums. It seemed with every wedding, young Michael's turn to play the drums extended. First it was one song and soon it became a full set. When the two men walked home, they always held hands, Grandpa was so proud and so happy. It was late for a young kid to be out even if it was a Saturday night. Arriving home, Grandpa closed the front door gently, and they quietly walked up the steps. He slipped Michael out of his clothes, carefully hung them up and put Michael to bed. A kiss on his forehead and he was soundly asleep. Grandpa looked down at Michael, the child may be a prodigy, but he was only four and needed rest and time to be a kid.

Tenderly kissing Julie, he remarked, "It was a wonderful wedding, lots of delicious food but the best part was when our grandson played an entire set with the band. I had tears in my eyes as everyone applauded little Michael. There are no words to describe how proud I am of Michael. Mark my words, he will become someone important and everyone will know his name."

"Husband, I believe you. Now, please get out of those clothes you have been wearing all day and take a shower," she instructed. He planted another kiss on her lips and disappeared into the bathroom. *Ahh, the luxury of a long warm shower!* A few minutes later he climbed into their bed and enjoyed a long restful night. In spite of the frigid rain, the Leonetti family trudged to church. Clutching several black umbrellas, they huddled together until reaching the church door. It was the typical sermon, accompanied by the usual walk home but that Sunday, routine was punctuated by a cold persistent rain. Michael raced up the front stoop and tried to pry the front door open, but his grandpa added that extra needed push and instantly the family was standing inside the small foyer.

One by one they hung up their coats removed their goulashes and began preparations for balance of the extended family who would be arriving in two hours. There were many firsts as a young child and that Sunday would mark another first for Michael. At four years old, he had shown interest in cooking and sporadically would assist his grandma in the kitchen. It was clear he loved the art of cooking; the smells, the preparations, the tasting and finally the eating.

"Michael, how about you join me in the kitchen and help me make Sunday dinner?" asked Julie.

Although he was used to practicing the drums, that was an offer he would not turn down. He ran upstairs stripped off his church clothes put on a tee-shirt and cotton pants, rambled down the steps and plunked himself next to his grandma. There was a metal stepstool in the kitchen. She moved it next to the sink, told Michael to wash his hands and they would begin preparing dinner for twenty people. His first job was to help make the meatballs, it was safe and didn't involve using a knife, that would come later.

Julie set a large wooden bowl inside the kitchen sink. Extracting a three-pound bag of ground meat from the refrigerator, she placed it on the countertop and asked Michael what he thinks he should do. Grabbing the bag, he opened it up, spread the meat into the bowl and pointed to the spice cabinet. One by one Julie took each condiment from a shelf, named it, made Michael repeat the name, and then allowed him to sprinkle some onto the meat.

Watching his every move she would halt him when he had added just the right amount. Opening his palms, he grabbed the meat and squished it in between his fingers, marrying the spices into the raw meat. Adding several other ingredients, he repeated the same mixing process and twenty minutes later the once bland ground meat had been turned into an explosion of flavors. Grabbing a roasting pan, Julie demonstrated how to roll the perfect meatball. Soon the entire tray was filled with identical meatballs and ready for the frying process.

Julie kissed Michael on the forehead, "Perfection," she pronounced. "Are you ready to learn more?" He bobbed his head yes and they began preparing lasagna.

Two hours later Michael emerged from the kitchen, happy, sweating and exhausted. He learned what went into all those Sunday meals and he couldn't wait to return for another try.

And another try he got as week after week Julie invited him into the tiny kitchen and taught him all her secrets and techniques. He never forgot anything and decades later he would pay homage to her patient lessons. After a scrumptious Easter Sunday dinner replete with a roasted lamb, colored boiled eggs and sausages, the grandparents made an announcement.

Grandpa raised his glass, "I would like to thank my wife and grandson for making another wonderful meal."

The guests raised their glasses and clapped. "To show my gratitude, I have planned a vacation. I have planned a trip to Miami. A little change of pace and scenery is good for everyone, even our grandson." "Your son is our grandson. We love him so much and want to show him as much of the world as we can. It's settled. Michael, you will take a real vacation with us and I promise you will love Florida," added Grandpa.

Chapter 4

SEEING THE WORLD MIAMI BEACH STYLE

The firsts continued for Michael. On that Wednesday morning it became his first airplane flight. Dolores, Aunt Elsie, and the Grandparents needed a vacation, it had been years since Grandpa Michael took time off from the florist business and relaxed. When he made the decision to go on vacation, he called an old friend and asked him to run the store for a week. Standing on the front stoop, the five huddled together with packed bags anxiously waiting for the taxi to arrive. The sky was littered with gray clouds promising a cold spring shower. Julie held Michael's hand, "Look at those ugly clouds, we won't see those in Florida."

The short ride to the airport was unremarkable as morning rush hour had ended and the roads emptied. The driver eased the cab up to the entrance, Grandpa paid him and retrieved the bags. They walked up to the ticket agent, checked the bags. followed the crowd through security and into the long corridor leading to the departure gate. Standing at the gate Julie looked around, "We are the first to arrive." Looking down at her grandson, "Your grandpa is always early and it seems as though today is no different. It will be almost two hours before our flight leaves."

They sat for a while and young Michael pointed to the planes landing and taking off. "Are we going in one of those?" he asked.

Julie said "yes."

"How do they stay in the sky?"

She didn't have the answer but, "the plane is like a big bird. Birds know how to fly and so do the pilots of these giant birds." For the moment that satisfied his curiosity or perhaps his fear. He continued looking out the huge glass window until rain began splashing and a fearful expression replaced his smile. Julie gave her spouse an irritated look, she knew it would difficult to keep their active grandson happy until it was time to board. Reading Julie's mind Grandpa grabbed his grandson's hand and suggested they investigate the airport. They enjoyed a slice of pizza and soda and meandered around the gift shop where Grandpa purchased several candy bars for the three-hour flight.

By the time they returned to the gate it was time to board. Julie clasped Michael's hand as they walked over the bridge and into the belly of the plane. Finding their seats at the back of the cabin, she helped him buckle the seatbelt.

Pointing to the various parts of the plane she had his complete attention which took his mind off any fears he might be harboring."This is your first flight, and you are going to love it," assured Julie. "Your grandpa and I have been on many flights and they have been wonderful. You'll see, you will love it too."

The door slammed shut and the drone of the engines escalated as the plane began taxiing on the tarmac.

The nose turned, pointing south, the engines roared to life and they lifted off the ground. The thump of the wheels curled up into the underbelly of the plane frightening Michael, but when they broke through the gray clouds and all he could see was sunlight, he relaxed.

"Isn't this beautiful? It's like we are close to heaven," said Julie. "We are flying like birds. You are right grandma this is fun."

The grandparents closed their eyes and fell asleep but Michael was mesmerized with the view from thirty-thousand feet above the ground and never took his eyes off the window. The sound of the pilot's voice announced they would be landing in sunny Miami and everyone should buckle their seatbelts.

Another first, Michael would experience the sight of seeing the ocean from the sky. Tugging on his Grandpa's arm he pointed to the aqua marine colored ocean. "Beautiful and warm," said Grandpa. "If you look closely, you can see fish jumping out of the water, there are a lot of dolphins."

Retracing their steps, they exited the plane, retrieved their bags, grabbed another taxi and stood outside a huge hotel situated on the beach. "Now I would say we are in heaven," remarked Julie. Pointing to the beach, "as soon as we get to our room we will change into swimsuits and go right to the ocean. It isn't like our ocean up north, it is warm and feels delicious." Michael didn't need any coaxing. As soon as the valet brought the bags into the spacious suite he disrobed, found a swimsuit and screamed, "Ready!"

The five vacationers walked down the hallway decorated in pastels, punched the elevator button and landed in the lobby. Turning to the left, they found a huge lagoon pool and reserved four loungers near the shallow end. Grandpa Michael took the room key and laid three huge white beach towels onto the loungers while Julie walked their grandson down to the beach.

"It's warm," he said. Letting go of her hand he ran to the edge of the ocean and splashed into the water.

"Grandma, you are right, the water is so warm. I can see the bottom!" She had never seen Michael so happy and carefree. Sometimes she forgot how young he was, so wrapped up in music, cooking and the world of adults, he had little time to act like a kid. The smile on his face said it all. Taking him on his first vacation was the right thing to do.

For dinner, they dined at the outdoor patio overlooking the ocean and soon after they returned to the room, promptly fell asleep to the soothing sound of the ocean waves beating against the shoreline. They were the five happiest vacationers in the world.

The next day Grandpa reserved the same loungers. After a long stroll on the beach, they returned to the pool and stretched out for a nice relaxing day. Michael didn't beg to go to the ocean.

There were tons of young kids frolicking in the pool and he was happy to make new friends and join in with the water games. There were several lifeguards who not only watched the young swimmers but kept them busy playing games which would eventually exhaust them.

Julie and Michael could truly relax, their grandson was in excellent hands. They spent the day drinking Mai Tais, eating fresh seafood, reading and napping. A perfect vacation!

Saturday morning Michael appeared lethargic. Grandpa touched his forehead and he was burning with a high fever.

He shook Julie, "Call down to the front desk and ask them to get us a cab to the nearest hospital." Throwing on a shirt, pants and sandals, Michael carried their grandson down the corridor and into a waiting cab. Julie knocked on Dolores and Elsie's room and nervously explained Michael's illness.

Five minutes later they were in a small emergency room filled with several other young children. What seemed like hours was only minutes until a nurse arrived and escorted them to a bed.

The nurse took Michael's temperature and vitals and instantly knew the problem. She had just treated a handful of patients with the same symptoms: meningitis a serious and sometimes fatal disease.

By now their happy child was crying and scared. The nurse hooked Michael up to an IV which contained numerous drugs and wheeled him to the pediatric floor. The terrified family trailed behind the bed.

When they reached the third floor the elevator slid open

and he was taken to a room in the far corner. The doctor arrived shortly after and explained the diagnosis and its severity. "We are doing all we can. For now, you will have to be patient and hopeful he will recover. I am not going to sugarcoat this disease, it can be fatal. Please remain calm and supportive." She abruptly left the room.

Julie and Dolores were hysterical but controlled their tears until they found the bathroom. The dream vacation had turned into a horrible nightmare. After shedding a stream of tears. they gathered some semblance of composure and returned to the room.

A moment later a nurse arrived. She had seen the worried look on family's faces, the terror that their child could die. It was part of her job to encourage and ease their concerns so they could in turn ease their child. After adjusting the IV line and adding additional drugs, she faced the family. "We are his grandparents," said Michael," and Dolores is his mom and Elsie is his aunt. This is our vacation and look where our grandson is?"

He started to sob so loudly the nurse told him to leave the room. "Come back when you have calmed down," she barked. Turning to Julie and Dolores she explained the disease and how the doctors treated the patients.

When she was finished, Julie said she understood. "I think you should wait another day. If his fever breaks by tomorrow morning he should be out of the worst of it. I can't tell you what to do but I think you should be patient, hold out for a day."

Julie shook her head in agreement, "Yes, I understand."

The nurse left the room promising to return within the hour. The arduous waiting began. Julie could hardly bring herself to look out the window and admire the ocean. She wasn't in the state of mind to admire anything. When she turned and observed her grandson lying comatose in the hospital bed it wasn't some whimsical dream it was reality. Trembling with fear, she clutched the gold cross dangling from her neck, sat down and prayed for a miracle, *bring my grandson back to me.* Dolores and Elsie paced the room, praying Michael would make it through. They were terrified. Young Michael's stay in the hospital lasted four long weeks before he showed any signs of regaining strength.

When the doctors gave the approval, Dolores and Elsie boarded a train and took Michael back home. The long ride home gave Dolores time to thank God for sparing her son and bringing him back to life.

The Leonettis' lives revolved around tradition especially the tradition of holidays. Michael looked forward to Christmas, his grandparents created a festive atmosphere which commenced the day after Thanksgiving. The presents, the decorations, special meals, music and family gatherings made this the major event of the year. He particularly looked forward to the appearance of Santa Claus and the presents left beneath the tree. Julie erected the metal tree the morning after Thanksgiving. Walking downstairs she pulled out a cardboard box that contained numerous pieces and year after year she assembled a small Christmas tree. What it lacked in authenticity was made up in decorations and dozens of elaborately wrapped gifts placed underneath the lowest bow. It stood in the corner of the living room and became the center of the Christmas spirit. Michael helped decorate. Bright glass bulbs, tiny colored lights and tinsel, lots and lots of tinsel.

The exterior of the house was flooded with strings of blinking lights. That was a busy time of year for the florist shop, between family gatherings, company parties, church services and funerals. Grandpa Michael was constantly busy creating arrangements. Julie loved the holiday as it meant more time with the family and a lot more time in the kitchen creating her famous meals. After the presents had been purchased, wrapped and placed under the tree, she began the task of cooking two major meals; Christmas Eve and Christmas Day. In the Catholic tradition, Christmas Eve was known as the Feast of the Seven Fishes. When the evening arrived, twenty-five close family members congregated in the grandparent's home to share the celebration. The front door was constantly opening and closing creating a draft of chilly winter air entering the foyer. Once inside, the atmosphere was as warm and toasty as a Caribbean island. Arms were brimming over with bottles of wine and gifts. The first floor of the house was so packed that the guests walked up a flight and placed their coats and boots in the bedrooms. The women were radiant in brightly colored dresses, the men in tweed jackets and cotton shirts and the children in velvet and red holiday sweaters. Grandpa Michael poured large glasses of wine for the adults and strawberry punch for the children.

Conversation flowed effortlessly, with smiles, looks of concerns, gentle touches, some kisses and a lot of hugs. Michael asked his Grandpa when they could open the presents. Glancing at his watch, he realized time had escaped him, it was getting late, "Soon but let's first play some music." Pushing back his chair he walked into the living room and pulled out a large vinyl record of Christmas music. The family adjourned from the table and moments later they were singing along.

Although they sang traditional holiday songs, Grandpa Michael led them in a few traditional Italian songs. Twenty-five strong, their voices pierced the third floor of the brownstone and into the heavens above. It was a truly memorable night.

"And now the presents," announced Grandpa Michael. The children sat uncharacteristically quietly as he handed out the brightly wrapped packages. Tearing open the paper, the kids were elated with their new toys. "It seems as though all of our children have been very good this year!"

Later that evening, after the guests had departed and Michael was tucked into his bed he heard something. Perhaps it was the sound of Julie walking up the steps but Michael's eyes flashed opened when he listened to a shuffling noise coming from the living room. Curious, he climbed out of bed, and crept down the steps. Right in front of his eyes he saw a large robust man in a red velvet suit. *He was all dressed in red, with a cap and a white beard and he was putting gifts under the Christmas tree. I was scared. I was five and the person was a stranger who somehow got into the house. I shrieked and ran up the steps and woke grandma.*

'You are dreaming, now go back to bed.' But I knew I wasn't dreaming, he was real as anything. I crept back down the steps and he had vanished but the gifts remained. I went back to bed and all I could think about was that I had been visited by an angel. That image has stayed with me since I was five years old and to this day, Christmas is my favorite part of the year.

After early morning mass, the extended family returned to the Leonetti home Christmas afternoon and gathered for another spectacular meal. Although there were numerous Italian dishes, Julie included a baked ham and roasted leg of lamb. The meal commenced with a spread of cold antipasto, followed by homemade roasted sausages, and a parade of pastas and roasted meats. Another memorable meal and another shared holiday. Family, it was all and always about family.

Chapter 5

School: I hated school

It wasn't that Michael was immature and couldn't face a day without his Grandpa and Grandma, it was that he felt like an adult trapped inside a child's body. He wanted to be with his grandpa, to play his music, listen to his advice and cook with his grandmother. School, that was for kids and Michael didn't feel as though he was a child. Dressed in a white shirt, dark cotton trousers and a navy tie, Grandpa escorted him to St. Nicholas and passed him off to the nuns. His first-grade teacher directed him to a desk near the back of the classroom.

Screaming all the way he finally calmed down and joined the ranks as a student "If you don't behave, the nuns beat the shit out of you," advised the boy seated behind Michael. Corporal punishment was implemented to keep unruly children properly behaved. The nuns made their students keep in line by using fear tactics and it worked, the students were terrified of their teachers and obeyed their every command. For Michael it was hell, he was used to being treated with love, and if he did something that his grandparents didn't approve of it was handled with a calm logical discussion. When the final bell of each school day rang, he was the first to burst from the doors and run into his grandparents arms. After a quick snack he would vanish to the basement and practice drums while his Grandpa assembled bouquets and funeral wreaths. They would talk about music, school and even business. After pondering the conversations with his grandfather, Michael became obsessed with making some money. He watched the men in the family making money and he wanted to emulate their behavior.

At the tender age of seven he began life as an entrepreneur as a shoe shine boy. For a nickel he would walk into bars and clubs with his box of supplies and hustle the customers. He was always welcome and learned how to shine shoes fast. Those coins began adding up quickly. When he had a few dollars, he walked to a local houseware store and purchased his mother gifts. He loved her so much and that was his way of demonstrating it.

Grandpa Michael funded his grandson's next venture; selling pretzels. Purchasing a wire basket and several containers of mustard young Michael walked the streets yelling "Pretzels, just a nickel." The only option was with or without a slathering of mustard. That turned out to be a great hit and he walked the streets for a year selling the delicious pretzels and saving his money. When Mother's Day and Christmas arrived he would be prepared, he could purchase his family gifts and for him that was a great feeling. Altruistic, even at seven, he thought of others and wanted to give back what they so generously gave him. He imagined their joy when opening beautifully wrapped gifts that he had purchased.

He fastidiously saved money, periodically purchasing gifts for his mother; a set of glasses, a toaster, or kitchen utensils. Unbeknownst to him, she would return the gifts and deposit the money into his savings account. Although she was appreciative of her son's acts of kindness, she knew one day Michael would need something and when that day arrived, the money would be available.

Grandpa was generous in sponsoring Michael's pretzel business but he was keenly aware of his grandson's talent as a drummer and wanted to support that endeavor. One afternoon he picked him up at school and they walked to Payne Music School. James LaPata was his teacher and began the formal process of teaching his youngest student about music. "I could never learn how to read music but it didn't matter. The teacher said show me what you can do. I would play and then he would demonstrate a technique and I would simply repeat what he did. After a while the teacher realized I didn't want to or need to read music that I could naturally hear the beats in the tunes.

For five years my music teacher tutored me in the art of drumming, he would listen, then demonstrate and I would copy. Music made me feel so happy, I would feel it inside my stomach. The rhythms made me feel high. The teacher would play all kinds of music and I would just naturally pick up on the beat and accompany the music creatively. My teacher was patient and praised me often. Despite the fact I never learned how to read music, I understood the music and that was enough for both me and my teacher," said Michael.

The five years of music lessons that Grandpa so happily paid for was an investment in Michael's future. He knew his grandson had raw talent, it just needed to be refined and the Payne Music School did just that. At ten, he was ready for his musical debut. The window in the cellar was wide open and the constant drumming sounds could be heard up and down the attached brownstones. A drummer needed a guitar, a keyboard, a real band. He sought schoolmates and bonded with three other friends naming the group, "Michael and The Bee Bops." The group consisted of brothers Phil and Frank Sabella, playing the accordion and guitar, and Daryl Depasqual, playing the bass guitar.

Together the foursome practiced in the basement until their sounds were perfected (at least good enough for the locals). Grandpa became the main source of the group's support. As a florist he was privy to upcoming events both good and bad, but it was the good events that allowed him to suggest using The Bee Bops for numerous occasions. He offered their services at a reasonable fee and became the group's booking agent. Each member of the group earned ten dollars for a booking. Their initial entrée into the world of performing was at Saturday night weddings. Michael had experienced the thrill of playing drums and now it was his band that would be the sole entertainment. Two weeks prior to their first performance, the band and their parents met at a tailor shop and purchased their first costumes. Simple, the jackets were light blue with black lapels, black pants and pristine white shirts. Standing shoulder-to-shoulder, the four pre-teens were cute with hopeful expressions on their faces. The night of their first gig, the heavy equipment was deposited into the back of the Sabella's station wagon. The four ten-year-old kids were driven a couple of blocks to the Catholic church. It took them nearly an hour to attach the various electrical cords and set up the instruments and when the bride and groom entered the catering hall, there was a loud crash of the cymbals and the music commenced. It was the boys good fortune that alcohol flowed freely that night and that they had selected just the right tunes to stir the guests. Booking the next gigs became easier for Grandpa Michael. The boyband looked great, four young kids with thick black hair, lanky bodies and broad smiles. It was obvious they were having as much fun as the guests.

Grandpa continued as their manager, booking the group at weddings, bar mitzvahs, and private parties, always making sure the boys were home before ten in evening. They were young, needed their rest and no matter what, when the bells chimed on Sunday morning, they all had to appear at mass.

The band became Michael's obsession, as it did for the other three members. They practiced faithfully in Grandpa's basement. No one in the neighborhood minded the cacophony, and it often served as an audition when a bride-to-be walked into the shop and ordered flowers for the up-coming nuptials. After overspending on flowers,

Grandpa would suggest the Bee Bops, "quite good, cute, and at ten dollars a head, you will save a lot of money." Another booking, another Saturday night, and another chance to expose their music.

As their talents improved, Grandpa booked the group at Jewish and Irish weddings. Grandpa realized to be successful, the boys needed to learn popular ethnic songs. He purchased records and helped them memorize the songs. They were pre-teens, had never escaped the neighborhood and had never heard any music other than what was on the radio or what they heard in church. It was eye-opening to expand their repertoire and it served to obtain more and more gigs.

Young Michael sought out the sounds of other bands, he wanted to hear other music, observe the reaction of the crowd and then take this knowledge back to his band. He would sneak into night clubs and listen to other bands. Seated at the back in a dark corner, he ordered sodas and listened intensively. Even as a pre-teen, he began to understand what it would take to become successful in the music business and devoted every free moment to making this happen. Unlike most kids his age, his musical tastes stemmed from the 40's and 50's, his passion was steeped in the crooners, the jazz musicians, and the classical melodies that are still performed today. He fell in love with that era of music, and it has remained with him ever since.

The boys stayed together and played together. Sometimes their pay was in sodas and roast beef sandwiches, and once they were paid in banana splits. They quickly outgrew their first costumes and were refitted into another identical set. Michael declared himself the bandleader, dictating the playlist and the way the music would be performed. He often battled the Sabella brothers who were more into current 60's music. But the reality was their gigs were at conservative events, they were not rock stars performing at a solo concert. Acquiescing to Michael's playlist, they played his choices plus special requests from the hosts of the events. Happy to perform and even happier when they were paid, the three members continued to follow Michael's directions (assisted by his doting Grandpa.).

Making memories for the guests at auspicious events was their goal but oftentimes it was the guests who created the memories. It had become the typical Saturday night wedding and on that mid-March evening they were playing at an Irish wedding. The bride was beautiful in her white gown, fire red flowing hair and emerald green eyes. There was a click of a highball glass and the room silenced as the father-of-the bride made the first toast. A few tears of joy were shed, the best man took the podium and offered his cheerful and humorous toast.

The father-of-the groom came next and rather than offering a toast nodded to the band and the musicians began playing *Danny Boy*. Inexplicably, the disturbing sound of glass shattering, broke the nostalgic moment, there was yelling and then two cousins stood and began punching each other. Beer bottles were chucked across the dance floor as Michael knelt behind his drum for protection. The other three boys fled the stage, hunkering next to the backdoor trembling with fear. A few moments later, there were slaps on the back, some laughter and the instigator yelled, "Play music!" Returning to the stage, the foursome finished out the evening. When the father-of-the-groom paid the group, he gave them each a nice tip, "Combat pay," he apologetically said.

The Bee Bops relentlessly practiced, refined their art, and expanded their playlist. Michael began to shine not only with his drumming but singing. Grandpa continued to act as advisor and suggested the boys enter local music contests, "It's a great way to get your name out there."

The Dante Theatre was the venue where they had seen dozens of movies, but it also served as a venue sponsoring local talent competitions. Grandpa entered the group in a contest and suggested they practice real hard. That they did and when the competition was completed, the winner was announced; it was the Bee Bops! Surprised, the group continued to enter the contests and they always won. It was a reinforcement that not only were they a great band, but the music and arrangements by Michael were highly touted, he had put them on the right track.

For Michael, it was the singing that became paramount. The group would meet for practice and seek out a place that had an echo chamber, sometimes it was a bathroom or an empty hall or a train station. They could listen to the notes reverberate and make corrections. They were those young kids singing harmony beneath the lamp posts, but they took their singing to another level. Good wasn't their goal, it was greatness they were seeking, especially

Michael. For him music was as natural as breathing, the rhythms, the melodies, flowed from him effortlessly. It was part of his soul. When he sang and played the drums his body was imbued with the music, his body and mind became completely immersed, it was almost as if the music hypnotized his very being. Euphoria best described Michael's relationship with music.

Chapter 6

MUSIC DEFINED LIFE

Loved by parents and grandparents, not only did Michael have natural talent but the support of an extended family. Confidence was a precarious human attribute but for Michael, he was blessed with a truck load. Undaunted, he would walk into clubs and bars, listen to the music and memorize chords, beats and lyrics.

Always seated in the back, he ordered sodas but as time progressed and his confidence level heightened, he thought he could get anything he wanted.

Dressed up in Sunday church clothes, he snuck into his mother's make-up drawer and painted a mustache on his upper lip. Convinced that would fool any bartender he saddled up to the local bar, ordered a beer and flirted with the girls. But the bartender wasn't as stupid as Michael was naïve and threw him out of the bar. "Next time your group comes into this place bring a chaperone," he screamed. Michael didn't get the beer, but he did get the girls.

The girls didn't seem to mind or care about his age. Attracted to his music and his good looks they were happy to accept a date. And so, he learned the ways of the dating world from those lovely older women.

Michael often remarked that he never felt like a kid, that he was born an adult in a kid's body. Not only was that apparent with his obsession for classical tunes but in the manner in which he carried himself and his choice of clothing. Upon entering high school, he traded in the Catholic uniform for a three-piece suit. When he walked the halls, his classmates mistook him for a teacher.

The principal was so annoyed that he called Dolores into his office for a conference. "The kid needs help," he insisted.

Dolores laughed, "You called me here to complain that my son is wearing a suit? Let him be, he is who is. Surely wearing a suit can't cause any harm to anyone."

"Except the students think he is a teacher and frankly he is a lot better dressed than our teachers. Can you ask him to tone it down? Please."

"My son thinks of himself as an old soul. He is a musician and this is part of his creativity. Instead of complaining about him, come and listen to the beautiful music he makes with his band. Perhaps that will change your mind."

Once the Bee Bops tasted playing in local bars, they began expanding outside the immediate neighborhood. Each new gig meant more people heard their music and more people became acquainted with their name.

As long as there was a chaperone, the band was welcome into clubs and bars. Experiencing the perks of adult venues, the boys only wanted to be booked in those places. It was the girls, the extra cash tips left on the floor and sometimes it was sneaking a beer. That added up to a lot more fun than playing at weddings. Some of the venues were rough, the Irish bars, the biker's clubs and the girlie clubs. The customers were mostly men, tough men who used the bars as an outlet to vent their anger or unhappiness at home. Tossing empty beer bottles was not uncommon, or a brawl between a couple of the guys. But always it was settled quickly, no one wanted the police to arrive to interrupt their beer drinking. Through it all the Bee Bops would play their music trying to avoid getting hit by a jettisoned bottle or worse, another person.

The once weekly gig expanded into a two-night gig, playing both Friday and Saturday nights. The group was now earning fifty dollars a person plus tips and all the sodas they wanted.

Their popularity escalated and Grandpa acted upon this. When the summer of their junior year arrived, he suggested the group explore Atlantic City. Unlike the clubs in and around Philadelphia, the group would be performing a show, actually two shows an evening, both ninety minutes each. That meant polishing their act, expanding the playlist and adding a little choreography. The boys were elated at the chance to perform in the famous resort town along with world-famous artists. They had long since dispersed with the accordion replacing it with keyboards Modern, they envisioned their names in lights on the marquees. That was a little overzealous thinking, they would be performing in clubs and showrooms where the not-so-famous artists were appearing. But for their young age, Grandpa was making sure they were getting exposure. After high school was adjourned for the summer, Grandpa and Julie drove the band down to Atlantic City.

A decade earlier, the couple had purchased a modest row house near the ocean, a respite from the hot summer humidity in Philadelphia. The house was shaped like a long, narrow and long and two stories. The top floor housed four bedrooms and the first floor, the one and only bathroom, a kitchen and living room. It was cozy, but they spent most of their time on the patio and boardwalk enjoying the cool breezes and ocean water. On that Friday morning, the boys arrived at the Leonetti house with their instruments, costumes and summer clothing. It was a lot of stuff, but Julie managed to arrange everything in the trunk, including Michael's drum set (which was disassembled). Julie slammed the trunk, the four boys squeezed into the back seat, Grandpa turned on the engine and off they went. Michael knew the trip by heart but this time it was fraught with anticipation, it was the first time the group would be performing in the world-famous resort town. The sixty-mile drive seemed like an eternity to the boys as they anxiously discussed their first gig.

The canopy of tall evergreens shaded the highway, thinning as the car turned directly eastbound and headed directly to the ocean. Low lying grasses lined the two-lane causeway, the sky was filled with puffy cumulus clouds, and the air smelled like salt; they had arrived at their destination. Julie's chest rose as she inhaled the fresh ocean air. Back home the smells were limited to whatever was cooking in the kitchen. In the summer the smells became trapped in the dense humidity and remained until a north wind or heavy downpour arrived and washed it all away.

At the beach, she felt alive and turning around looking at the kids in the back seat, it seemed as though they felt the same way. Their broad smiles, fingers pointing to sea gulls flying by, and the "wow" sounds when they saw the blue ocean waters displayed their excitement. No doubt they loved the beauty of the coastline as much as she.

Hundreds of beach bungalows and small mom and pop stores were bunched along the shoreline. A mile north, the bustling boardwalk, smaller nightclubs, eating establishments and at the end, an amusement park was built on a pier extending over the water.

The salty smell of the ocean air was intoxicating but it was the massive ocean with its perpetual ebb and flow of the tide that made Atlantic City famous. The beachfront was wide with clean white sand and when the ocean slapped onto the shore, the sand was cool and easy to walk on.

Julie pointed out a few of the sites and then Grandpa eased the car into the last spot on the side street, thirty paces from their summer home. The boys sprung from the back seat, stretched, and immediately emptied the trunk into the row house. Julie directed them to their bedrooms and insisted the band equipment remain in the living room so they could easily practice. "I know you are used to our basement, but here, you will have command of the living room. That way all the neighbors can hear your music and come to your shows. You kids unpack and I will make us lunch," said Julie who had a hungry audience for whatever would emerge from the kitchen. Grandpa was busy making last minute details for the group's first performance. Everyone in the household was engaged in activity, excited and hopeful.

For once Grandpa took over the dinner meal, steaming delicious crabs, a local favorite. Before the boys' first performance, he cooked a pot of Maryland crabs, with a side of pasta, and set the table with a huge pitcher of water. They ripped the crustaceans apart, devouring every morsel. Grandpa showed the boys the art of sucking every bit of meat from the claws. They loved the meal and begged for more.

"Another night," he promised. Julie smiled, she had to admit it was a nice change of pace to let someone else inside her kitchen and it was even nicer when her spouse washed the dishes, poured a brandy and suggested they sit on the beach. With blanket in hand they strolled to the ocean front, sipped on the brandy and remembered why they fell in love. The waxing moon provided just enough light, casting a shadow on the ocean waves. Michael wrapped his arms around Julie, kissed her and held her for hours. He never took her love for granted, she was an angel and had given him the best years of his life. There was a lot to look forward to, life with Julie was as happy and fulfilled as he ever imagined and they would have many years ahead to love and live and enjoy their blessings.

The Coliseum, a long-established night club on the boardwalk, featured an ad in the local paper showing Michael playing the drums labeled the group as "The Leonetti Show." Although the three other musicians were happy to be performing, using only Michael's name as the headliner caused a rift in their relationship, one that had been building for a while. The Sabella brothers, wanted to play more current cover tunes, but Michael's mind was trapped in the earlier decades.

That evening showtime was from nine o'clock to two in the morning. For once, none of the boys would rise early for Sunday morning mass, they would be sound asleep. Julie and Grandpa Michael stayed for most of the show, driving home well before it ended. The boys eventually walked home, exhausted but thrilled with the reception they received from a rotating audience. The tip jar was over-flowing and the manager went out of his way to thank the group. "I'll be in touch with your manager and see you soon."

Four exuberant young men were at the birth of their careers, they were beyond happy. When they walked along the boardwalk, girls in the audience recognized the performers and would run up to them and flirt. The attention was an added perk to becoming a well-known performer, now all they had to do was keep the momentum going. That was left to Grandpa Michael, the man with a plan. For the band, the two weeks in Atlantic City was filled with practice, enjoying the beach, and performing at night. For Grandpa it was filled with planning more gigs and enjoying some relaxing time with his wife.

Listening to the gently rolling waves Michael pondered his future and all he could visualize was playing music, it was the only thing that made him happy, truly and completely. It had been that way since he was four years old and he knew that path would never change.

Soon the group would pack and leave, and he wanted to know what Grandpa had in mind for the rest of the summer. He didn't want to keep replaying the memories at the Coliseum, he wanted that opportunity to begin launching his career outside the city of Philadelphia.

Julie had efficiently repacked the car for the ride home. In the front seat she held a large bag filled with sodas, sandwiches and chips. She didn't want anyone starving on the sixty- mile trip home. The mood in the back seat was much different returning home. Fears and anxiety were replaced with a sense of accomplishment of a gig well done. Grandpa interjected endless kudos, how the group had wowed the crowds, how the showroom manager was thrilled with the reception. The group attracted a younger crowd, barely legal, and they loved to drink, receipts were up when the Bee Bops were on center stage.

"Grandpa," said Michael, "The sound of the sax really made a difference in the music. It added that jazz sound and I guess the customers liked it." No one could deny that fact, although the Sabella brothers still held to their guns, only wanting to play current top forty hits.

"We can play it all," they said. Arriving back home, Grandpa parked the car near the front of the brownstone and they all piled out.

"Rehearsal at noon tomorrow," Michael reminded, "and (looking directly into his Grandpa's eyes), we will go over the list of gigs for the rest of the summer. The three boys carted their instruments into the basement, grabbed their bags of dirty clothing and walked home.

The basement was cooler than the first floor of the brownstone, but it was still hot and the humidity was nearly eighty percent. Sweat was dripping from every pore as the four musicians practiced a new song. They had to learn how to incorporate the sound of the saxophone with the guitars. Sometimes Michael would get up and stand in front of the three musicians and listen. So attuned to nuances in rhythm and chord structure, he knew when to make just the smallest of adjustments to enhance the song.

Wiping sweat from their foreheads, they decided to take a ten-minute break. While gulping bottles of soda they heard the familiar footsteps of Grandpa walking down the cellar steps. In his hand was a wrinkled piece of paper, "Your set of gigs for the next few weeks," he proudly announced. And the whirlwind commenced, at places they had never played; Camelot, Porter House, 13th Street Lounge, Sportsmen's Tavern, Roche Post, The Wyoming Lounge, Salvatore's Restaurant, Vira De Reitti, Red Chimney, Marco's, T R Club, and Gigi's. Those venues were a step up and a far cry from the local Irish and biker bars.

At these up-scale venues, when they played, the audience listened, and never threw bottles or punches. The stage was theirs and the customers paid homage with loud applause and return visits. The boys learned how to bow and return the crowd's response, that was the easiest part of the performance and the most gratifying. At these gigs they were paid in cash, maybe they were served a plate of pasta but it was in addition to the money.

As the summer progressed and Michael's singing improved to star quality, he and Grandpa discussed a trip to Florida, Miami Beach. Grandpa had a lot of connections and although Michael was very young, his talent was ready to be tested in the waters of finicky Southern Floridians. After making a series of calls, he was booked for three weeks at four-star hotels. The Fontainebleau welcomed his entrée and was looking forward to showing off a new fresh talent.

When his flight was announced, Michael walked confidently down the gangplank, took his seat buckled his seatbelt and rechecked his wallet. It was there, right where he put it, a fake identification card. He took a chance no one would check his age, his resume certainly screamed older than a teenager and now with this card, he could enjoy a beer and perhaps a babe. He was fully prepared for Miami Beach! This would be the very first time he fully broke away from his band, the marquee read, Michael Leonetti. There was no band name, it was his name and his name alone. He would go solo, the spotlight was only on him.

Chapter 7

LAS VEGAS A PLACE TO MAKE IT REAL

Another first for Michael was driving thousands of miles across America. The farthest he had traveled was Florida but he had flown to that destination. The car was a symbol of permeance, he had made a decision and now he, with his few possessions and Billy would be creating their future. He had been with the Bee Bops for fifteen years and finally he was spreading his wings.

He met Billy in Atlantic City and they became fast friends. When Michael decided to move to Las Vegas Billy was excited to join him. Reviewing the road maps, Billy plotted the route, while Michael did most of the driving. They talked endlessly about performing, where they would live, how they would get gigs, the babes, the casinos, and life in the hot sunny desert. No more snow falls or cold endless rainy days. They envisioned the city streets paved with gold, the sky always sapphire blue, and their apartment spacious. What they envisioned was nirvana.

The Oldsmobile easily negotiated the highways and the windy mountain route and four days later as the sun was setting behind Red Rock Mountains, they recognized the silhouette of Las Vegas. Turning south onto Las Vegas Boulevard, they were amazed at the thousands of lights lining the street. The massive marquees announced the performers, Keno deals, huge buffets and cheap luxury rooms.

Michael's heart pounded with excitement and anticipation as they slowly continued driving south on the strip. It seemed as though the casinos went on forever. It was a gigantic town, "There is plenty of room for us in this place," he announced. "Just look at the endless line of casinos, hotels, restaurants and shops. We could play a different gig every night for a year and still have new places to play."

That was the early 1970s when international celebrities came into the city to entertain, they paved the streets with gold, enticing tourists around the world. The Rat Pack, the best of the best performed in the major casinos, Frank Sinatra, Dean Martin, Sammy Davis Jr., and Andy Williams. The city was a magnet attracting the most renown performer artists in the world.

Billy agreed. It was one thing to dream of coming to Las Vegas but quite another thing to actually be there and witness firsthand the huge opportunities for two young performers. "A place to stay," Billy said. Laying down the map, he peeked in between the large casinos and noticed several stout buildings lining the streets behind the main drag. "Over there," he pointed.

Michael waited at the traffic light and made a left turn eastward. Numerous small signs advertised cheap luxurious apartment living. Pulling the car into the Shadow Apartments they walked into the rental office.

Monthly rates were one-hundred-twenty dollars and for ten bucks more, they could rent a two-bedroom apartment, fully furnished. Forking over the first month rental money, the clerk handed over two keys and wished them luck. Parking the car under the covered port, they lugged up the contents of the trunk, took quick showers and walked to the strip. "Food." Strolling along the sidewalk, they found a burger joint. Ordering two beers, burgers and fries, they sat watching the throngs of people strolling along the strip. Although it was early September and the eastern seaboard was bracing for a hurricane, the weather in the desert was dry and hot. The one thing the city could count on was spectacular weather, it was either hot and sunny, warm and sunny and in the dark days of winter, cool and sunny. Rarely did a day pass when the sun wasn't shining. Dusk provided a lingering view of the setting sun sinking against the low Red Rock Mountains. Beauty was everywhere. The landscape provided an unusual look into Mother Nature, with unique flora and fauna indigenous only to desert life.

After eating, Billy and Michael joined the crowds strolling the strip. It was startling to see so many people having fun, it was as if the city was giving a party for the world. On each corner they heard voices reflecting foreign countries around the globe. The vacationers arrived to have the time of their life and the casinos made sure they didn't disappoint. These two talented men would be a part of making the city great, they would perform their music and make the audiences cheer for more.

Michael and Billy had big dreams, they wanted gigs in the main showrooms. They came to Las Vegas to make themselves famous and refused to settle for anything less. At twenty-one, they had plenty of time to make that happen. But that dream of performing in the main showrooms translated into elaborate costumes, dancers and charts for the orchestra, which translated into having a pool of cash. Pondering the situation, Michael sought a job which would immediately bring in the needed cash. Walking along the boulevard, he noticed a large restaurant, The Tower of Pizza, right up his alley. It was early in the day and there were a few customers sipping coffee and reading the local newspaper. Michael boldly walked towards the kitchen and asked to meet the manager. He didn't have a resume, he had a heritage, an Italian culture engrained in his heart and soul. Introducing himself, he began explaining the magic he could perform in the kitchen. People like Michael didn't walk into this establishment every day of the week, the manager sensed the kid had a special talent for bringing out the best in a clove of garlic.

"I'll give you a try," said the manager, "Can you start tomorrow?"

"Tomorrow?" answered Michael, "How about today?"

"Okay, I will put you to work." Thus, began the start of his professional cooking career. Jasper was the owner and when he saw a new chef in the kitchen he was curious.

Asking Michael to cook up some Italian specialties when the plate was placed on the table the aroma was truly authentic. One bite and Jasper knew that kid knew how to cook. By the end of the second week, Mafia characters sauntered into the restaurant and began enjoying the food, "Just like mom used to make, God rest her soul."

"Who is the new cook?" they asked. Michael would walk out from the kitchen, shake their hands and thank them for coming into the restaurant. One day he was brave and summoned up the courage to provide more than just food. After the meal was served, he began singing, *My Kind of Town*. All faces in the bustling restaurant turned and observed the cook belt out the tune. Applause rang out and Michael took his first bow as a chef. Young and naïve, he had no idea that the Mafia clientele could help boost his career. They fell in love with his food and later, his voice. Handing him slips of paper with names and phone numbers, the gigs came easier to book. Soon, he and Billy were busy most every night performing.

Billy took over as music director coordinating the play list, setting the stage, obtaining back-up musicians and ever-searching for a manager who could catapult them to fame.

He walked the streets, talked to agents and found a manager who knew the ropes, Roy Paratore. Roy's main job was construction but he knew the right people and opened doors for Michael. Italians stuck together and helped each other. With two young talented boys from Philadelphia, it was easy to sell their show. Handsome, vibrant and bubbling over with passion, their performances attracted customers. Once tourists heard Michael sing, many stayed for both shows. Billy had gathered a vast amount of sheet music and when Michael offered to sing special requests, he was able to appease customers from many walks of life. Once in while a Jewish, Italian or Irish song would be requested and Michael would recall the tune he had sang at weddings. It was those special songs that added extra cash in the tip jars.

Six months later, Billy and Michael moved into the Egyptian Apartment complex. Two blocks east of the strip, the two-bedroom, two-bathroom apartment was spacious, with an outdoor pool and jacuzzi.

The move into the new apartment was simple. With few possessions, three round trips with the Oldsmobile and they were installed into their new living quarters. There were always a spat of young men and women lounging around the pool, it became the simplest way to make friends. Monday was the only day of the week he didn't work and Michael used it to cook up a storm of Italian food. The smell wafted through the open sliding glass door attracting people to his apartment. His reputation rapidly spread and soon the apartment was filled with young men and women. He would serve up great food and the guests would bring wine and beer.

Billy was in charge of the music and made sure there was always a record spinning. It didn't take long for the two young men to make a large group of friends. With a full refrigerator, and a stocked bar, their social life rapidly expanded. One evening after the party finally broke up, Billy turned to Michael and asked him if he was homesick. Since the moment they drove out of Philadelphia, neither had mentioned a word about missing family and friends. All their discussions centered around their futures, the life they would create using their talents. Michael missed his family, his son, Michael, and his friends, but it never clouded his mind nor made him long for his old life. He had made mistakes and was ready to move on. What he wanted would never had come to fruition had he remained in the Italian neighborhood.

"Billy, I am genuinely happy to be in Las Vegas and happy you took a chance on me. It wasn't so easy to leave home and I have never really thanked you for coming along on this unpredictable adventure."

"You know what? I am truly happy. I never would have come on my own. I love it here, the gigs, the friends, the life style. For me it's as close to heaven on earth as it gets," said Billy.

And for the two men, they lived an enviable life, performing at night, meeting people from around the world, sampling new foods, new music, and new places to live. As drawn as they were to many new experiences, others were drawn to them. Michael's cooking became legendary at The Tower of Pizza, earning him the respect of powerful men who helped him achieve his dream as a headliner. Billy's good looks, musical talent and ability to conduct a top-notch show, drew talent agents, assuring their music would be heard.

The city was divided into downtown, Fremont Street, and the southern strip which was lined with newer resorts. Every hotel-casino housed lounge acts and some luxurious showrooms. Michael booked gigs on the southern strip at The Sahara, Caesars, MGM, The Thunderbird, The Flamingo, The Tropicana and downtown at Golden Nugget, The Mint, Fremont, and Four Queens.

The contracts ran a few weeks and they would move on to the next venue. After they had exhausted first runs they would begin again. The Leonetti name became well-known in the lounge circuit. When the time finally arrived to headline a showroom, Billy was able to make it happen.

Michael selected the costumes and the playlist and Billy was the music director, in charge of making sure all the charts (sheet music) for the orchestra were properly prepared. He knew how to read and write music and was technically prepared for the challenging job.

Their opening was a Friday night in the dead of winter, when the rest of America was suffering with snow and brutally cold temperatures. Tourists swarmed to Las Vegas to warm their bones, fill their stomachs, gamble, shop, and be entertained.

Billy entered the stage, warmed up the band, the lights faded and a single spotlight followed the singer to center stage. A dramatic pause, a long breath and Michael began. Singing from his soul, he touched the hearts of the audience. Two ballads into the first show loud applause rang out and several tables stood clapping. Tears welled in the corners of his eyes, he knew he held the audience in the palm of his hand. Thanking the crowd, he nodded to Billy and the music continued until ninety-minutes vanished. The hotels had strong rules and one of them was keeping the show on schedule, they needed the audience back inside the casinos, gambling, drinking and spending lots of money. Billy always abided by the rules, he knew the consequences would mean banishment. They were just getting started in their careers and wanted to appease the powerful management.

With his arms outstretched, Billy brought down the baton, the music ceased and the stage lights went dark. The show was over and on time.

Those tears that Michael shed in mid-performance blossomed as he hugged Billy. "We did it! Did you hear the applause, see their smiles? Did you watch as they sung along? Did you see them stand?"

Overcome with joy, he felt as if he were sailing in the sky, floating above the earth. Returning to the dressing room, they changed clothing and entered the casino.

As they walked through the crowds clustered around table games, many turned around and congratulated the performers on a great show. Another confirmation their talents were appreciated.

Chapter 8

The evolution of entertainment

Life continued on an even keel, Michael held down his day job and performed in the evenings.
Getting gigs became more difficult as the casinos morphed from individual ownership to corporations. Every penny was counted, as the casinos now had to answer to a board of directors and stockholders. Getting rid of excess spending was principal in the running of the businesses. One of the ways management cut corners was lowering the entertainment expenditures. The lounge acts were changed from two shows nightly to sets played throughout the evening. The schedule became grueling for the entertainers while the fees dropped. Michael was burning the candle at both ends but at least he was performing, doing what he came to Las Vegas to do.

Michael performed his first show as a headliner with his name on the marquee and a sixteen-piece orchestra, the year was 1974. It was at the Marina Hotel and Casino.

He didn't just walk into the showroom, shake hands with the entertainment director and obtain a six-month gig. Not quite. It took a lot of time and cajoling the entertainment director to make that happen.

He saw his name on the marquees of the Dunes and later The Riviera. He would become a household word in Las Vegas and for those who visited the city and watched him perform, they carried his name in their minds and hearts, never forgetting his spectacular performances. The hotels made money when the Leonetti name was plastered on their marquees, it was guaranteed that every show would sell out and with it plenty of liquor would be consumed and the gambling tables filled. Michael went all out for these two casinos, with new charts, costumes, playlists and choreography. When he appeared he didn't want to repeat the same show for fear of losing repeat customers.

The second show was introduced onto the strip, it was touted as a brand new show with new songs and a full review. Success at both venues landed Michael into other competing venues. He had a proven track record, one that spun his reputation as a top tier entertainer and remained so for two decades.

It was one of the most prestigious lounge shows in Las Vegas, The Mint, a casino, in the heart of Fremont Street. The year was 1976 and Michael was the main artist in the lounge. One flight up was the showroom where world-famous acts performed, it was not unusual to see the likes of Cornell Gunter's Coasters, Little Anthony or the Rat Pack, walking up and down the steps performing in the two venues. On that Saturday evening, it was The Leonetti Show. Singing his heart out, the audience was thoroughly enraptured with the music. In the middle of the second set there was a commotion at the back of the room. Michael looked up and noticed a person in a gorilla suit clutching a bouquet of balloons, calling out a woman's name. The gorilla began singing Happy Birthday. Michael was annoyed, *how dare anyone walk in and ruin his show*? He turned to the musicians and held up his arms so they would stop playing, grabbed the microphone and shouted to the lighting director to put the spotlight on the gorilla. Once Happy Birthday was sung, the gorilla disappeared but not so with Michael's embarrassment.

"If I were Frank Sinatra, and the gorilla did this to me, I'd turn this lounge into a pizzeria." Shortly after the scene, Mike Mallone called Michael over and handed him a check for two weeks and told him to leave the casino. It turned out that Andrew Zorni, the hotel manager decided to fire Michael for his incendiary remarks, entertainers were not allowed to make negative statements regarding the running of the casino in front of an audience. Curious, Michael wanted to meet Mr. Zorni. He walked over to the pit behind the crap table and asked to meet the manager.

Two huge bouncers came over, physically picked up Michael and deposited him outside the casino on the sidewalk. As they were carrying him out the guy in the gorilla suit yelled out, "I'm sorry for ruining your show." Needless to say, The Leonetti Show, never graced the Mint lounge ever again.

Dusting himself off, he removed his jacket, tossed it over his left shoulder and walked home. Mulling over the scene, he realized that as a young performer, new to the Las Vegas circuit, he had acted rashly. Young, impetuous and inexperienced he felt he had to defend his talent, he did it the only way he knew how. It wasn't like he could draw on a history of experiences. Up until his move to Las Vegas, the worst that had ever happened was a few beer bottles slug his way.

That was not the end of his career, just the end of his career at The Mint.

Feeling down, the next morning Michael drove his trusty Oldsmobile to a dealership and traded it in for a shiny new black Cadillac. On the way home he felt so happy and proud to be driving this great new car he could hardly wait to go for a long drive.

At the apartment complex, he met Diane, sweet, demure and a good person inside and out. Raised with true Christian values, she knew right from wrong and acted accordingly. Thoughtful, she was altruistic, caring for others. She was always touting a gift or care package for a friend and she never forgot birthdays, anniversaries or holidays. Like Michael, Christmas was her favorite time of year. She loved the gift giving, the parties and the time with family and friends. She knew Michael was very close with his family and missed them especially around the holidays so she went out of her way to include them in their plans. He called home often and she would grab the phone and talk with Dolores and Louis. She purchased birthday gifts and dropped them off at the post office. Michael's family was important to her and she hoped one day they would be her in-laws. He would eventually make Diane his wife.

After years behind a hot stove, temperamental customers and long hours, Michael grew tired of cooking at the pizza restaurant and decided to try another profession. He wanted and needed to make more money. The nightly gigs were become farther and farther apart and neither his manager nor his friends could alter the tide the casinos were turning. He began searching for another job and took a position selling timeshares.

The job offered a base salary but the majority of his income was derived from commissions. His job was to entice tourists into reviewing the possibility of owning a timeshare. Dozens of facilities were being built on the southern end of the strip as well as other resort destinations around the world. With his outgoing personality, it seemed an excellent fit. He no longer worked on Monday and Tuesday but put in long hours from Wednesday to mid-Sunday afternoon.

It took him little time to become one of the top salespersons. He knew how to sell and how to entice people to listen to his sales pitch. When all else failed, he pulled out all the stops and sang his way into people's purse strings. Dressing in resort clothing he stood in lobbies and handed out pamphlets hoping to pique the interest of a passing tourist just enough to observe a short video and hear the sales pitch. Because so many of the timeshares were being built right in Las Vegas, it was a short drive to see the complexes.

Once the potential buyers saw the resort campus it became even easier to sell them. The buildings were state-of-the-art resort style living with lush landscaping, roomy apartments and resort amenities such as lagoon pools, gyms, poolside bars, and nightly entertainment. A tour through the property and the timeshare was sold. He became so adept at selling, his company moved him to other destinations such as San Diego, the Caribbean, and San Francisco. He would stay for a month to six weeks during high tourist season and sell the newest facility. He was at the right place at the right time, that was the beginning of the massive timeshare business and Michael knew how to seal a deal.

When the timeshare company offered Michael a trip to Hawaii for a month of selling, he grabbed the phone and called his wife. A chance for a real honeymoon. Although he would be working, there would be plenty of time together. Diane's boss was understanding and allowed her a week off. On Saturday evening, they caught the red eye to Honolulu, arriving as the sun was rising on the eastern Pacific. Taking a taxi to the property, the manager met them in the lobby and escorted the couple to a luxurious suite with a western view of the ocean. Handing Michael a pamphlet, and two keys, she told him to take the day off, wander around the resort and get to know the amenities

Chapter 9

Timeshares kept the finances in the family solvent but when sales began to slow, in 1990, Michael set his sights on alternative locations. He had traveled to numerous resort destinations around the globe and when a position opened in Lake Havasu, Arizona, he applied for the job. The resort was the Ramada Inn, directly south, two hours from Las Vegas, not a bad commute. It was famous for the London Bridge which was dismantled and brought to the city by Robert McCulloch. The resort, known only for its delightful lake, welcomed the idea of adding a world class attraction. The lake along with the bridge created a true resort destination and attracted thousands of tourists to the small desert town.

Thomas Flatey, owner of Ramada, bought the hotel and proceeded to upscale every inch of the grounds; from the pool, to the restaurants, redecorating the lobby, adding new linens, widening the parking lot, embellishing the landscaping and upgrading the signage. It was ready for a top-notch marketer. After reviewing Michael's resume, the owner was convinced he would be an excellent fit. Not only could Michael sell time shares, but entertain the tourists and add his input into the restaurant. With the expanded parking lot there was ample space to insure the refurbished restaurant would stay busy every night. And, Michael could cook. A man of many accomplishments, Thomas welcomed him to the staff and provided him with a suite. There was plenty of room for Diane and their baby, Elaina. On Michael's days off he would drive up to Las Vegas and on the weekends his family would come to visit. The town was beautiful and there were endless things to see and do: Rotary Park, London Bridge, dozens of unique shops, eateries, boating and natural wildlife tours, the aquatic center, museums, lighthouses, and endless water sports. While Michael was busy selling timeshares during the afternoons, Diane and Elaina had plenty to do to keep themselves busy. In the evenings when Michael was entertaining, they had front row seats, enjoyed a great meal and were blessed to watch Michael doing what he loved the most, singing and entertaining.

Paradise did not last forever

Michael had a big responsibility, selling timeshares was a delicate process and every step of the way meant excellent customer service. It was a highly competitive market. When Caroline, his secretary, was rude to customers he had no choice but to fire her. They fought and she denied she had been rude and callous, yet he had overheard her remarks and other employees concurred with her unprofessional behavior. The city was small and being fired from a resort was a blackmark on her resume.

Michael didn't care, his livelihood was on the line and his family and the business came first. With more than enough justification, he called her into his office and let her go. Caroline was mad as hell and had few alternatives for employment in a town that was barely twenty-five thousand people. She would make him pay. She went to the police and stated that he had fondled her breast.

Michael expeditiously hired the best lawyer in the city and the entire allegation was reduced to a non-sexual misdemeanor. Caroline's goal would have been to be bought off, but she underestimated Michael. The entire allegation evaporated into nothing and she looked like a lying fool. Her idea of revenge backfired and made her even more unlikely to be hired by anyone in the city. No employer wanted an employee who would lie out of revenge because she lost her job. Lake Havasu was and still is a small town and when an outsider arrived and was accused of wrongdoing it was publicized.

The front page of *The Herald,* the local paper, showed a photo of Michael with a headline reading, *Accused Breast Fondler.* Michael was devastated. He went to Thomas Flattery's office and offered to resign but the owner would not hear of it. He deflected Michael's worries with the fact that Michael was hired to turn the resort around and that translated into stepping on some toes and in that woman's case, it meant putting up with a revengeful scorned woman.

The newly refurbished showroom was prepared and

the premiere show featuring Michael Leonetti turned disastrous when the article hit the front page of the newspaper. The five-hundred seat theatre had presold only fifteen tickets. Michael was mortified. His debut was set for failure. Luckily, he had friends in the entertainment business and when he placed a call to Rich Little, the comedian was happy to oblige an old friend. Rearranging the lettering on the marquee, adding Rich Little's name to the line up alongside The Leonetti name, altered the course of success. The show was completely sold out and when Michael took his final bow, the audience stood and loudly applauded. That was the last time Michael had to rely on a friend to save the show. The residents of the city dismissed the allegations and the showroom was packed for the duration of the year. It would take more than one woman's lies to destroy Michael and his longtime career.

After a year, Michael, who had sold out the timeshares, packed his bags and returned to Las Vegas. One way or another, it was time to leave the town. A sorry lesson for firing an inept employee, he would carry that lesson in the back of his mind forever.

Chapter 10

DIANE'S ILLNESS

She had always been plagued with migraine headaches. Michael loathed observing his wife suffer and together they sought every known recourse. They traveled to San Diego and none of the specialists could alleviate her pain. Ironically the only time she didn't suffer from migraines was during her pregnancy.

After San Diego, they returned home feeling discouraged and helpless. Her pain continued and she made an appointment with her doctor who ordered another series of tests. He reserved a room at the hospital. The tests were evasive and he wanted to make sure she was watched around the clock. A surgeon would do exploratory surgery, this would be both painful and dangerous. When the doctor reviewed the results, he immediately punched the elevator and entered the hospital room. With a somber demeanor, he explained there was a cancerous mass around Diane's heart, that it was inoperable. Her only hope was chemotherapy. Surgery to remove the entire mass was not an option, one tiny nick on the aorta and her heart would stop.

Michael refused to believe that she had cancer and refused to allow the doctor to treat her with chemotherapy, a grueling long set of painful injections that could kill his wife He answered for his wife, "No, no to chemo. She doesn't have cancer!"

Storming out of the claustrophobic room, he paced the hallways insanely worried. Then he remembered an old friend. Grabbing his cell phone, he called Eddie, and asked for his valued advice. "Use these doctors Shoemaker and Jacobson." Michael immediately dialed the number and spoke to the nurse who appreciated the severity of the situation. She paged one of the doctors and advised Michael to transfer Diane to Sunrise Hospital. The nurse would call ahead and have a room waiting.

Trembling, Michael raced back to the room, fired the staff, collected Diane's possessions, wrapped her in a warm flannel robe and drove her to Sunrise Hospital. She trusted her husband's instinct and followed his lead. They sat in silence on the short ride to the next hospital, both in shock and worry.

Approaching the registration desk, Michael gave the intake receptionist Diane's name and she was ushered in a wheelchair to the surgical floor where they patiently waited for the arrival of the next team of doctors. Lying comfortably in a hospital bed, Michael turned on the television to divert his wife's mind.

His phone rang and he anxiously retrieved it from his jacket. "This is Dr. Bill Marranon," said the voice, "I was the surgeon who operated on your wife and was instructed that you fired me and the entire staff." "Yes," answered Michael. "I am so very sorry. But please listen to reason and give me another chance. If you would allow us to treat your wife with chemo it would give her a chance to live," the doctor pleaded. "No," Michael stated emphatically, "You will not treat her with chemo. I will not allow you to do that." He hung up the phone and never spoke with the doctor again.

Diane spent the night in the hospital and the next morning Michael returned with their daughter and a clearer head. Her parents were seated, each wearing worried expressions and staring into their daughter's face.

I took one look at my wife's face and felt the presence of the Angel of Death hovering in the room. The far away look on her face reflected a body that was ready to give itself to heaven. Her breathing was shallow and her skin was ashen, she was listless. It was the exact expression my dad wore just before he passed.

Michael sat on the edge of the bed and took Diane's hand, "Honey, they have to operate again."

She looked into her husband's eyes and pleaded, "I can't take the pain."

"They have to, it is the only option," he explained.

The nurse arrived, added a drug to the saline drip and moments later Diane fell sound asleep. Michael got up, explained to his daughter he had to leave for a while, kissed Elaina on the forehead and walked out of the hospital.

It was at St Vitor's Church that Michael made a pact with his Lord. Walking purposefully up to the water font, he dipped his forefinger into the water, crossed himself and continued walking to the first pew. A group of votives and sprays of sunlight flowing through the stain-glass windows provided the only illumination while he pondered the inexplicable. Looking around, Michael was assured he was alone and would have God's full attention. Not a praying man, he knelt and asked God to take him, not his wife.

The next morning the doctors arrived, explained the procedure and wheeled Diane into the operating room. Michael, his daughter and Diane's parents sat in the waiting room filled with trepidations. They paced, drank coffee, ate donuts, and sat mutely for hours. Finally, both doctors emerged behind the doors and made the announcement, "We found no cancer. There is nothing wrong with your daughter. As soon as she recovers from the surgery, she is good to go home and put this all behind her."

"What?" screamed Michael, "Are you saying that she never had cancer?"

"We can't answer for the other doctors, or what they saw. All we can tell you is that she is cancer free and is as healthy as any women her age."

Elaina jumped for joy, her mother was going to live! Diane's parents shed tears of joy. Michael stood, looked up at the ceiling and thanked God for saving his wife. A shudder snaked through his body, God was sending him a message, he was just too distracted to pay attention.

A few days later, Diane was home and getting back to her routine, caring for Elaina, working at the newspaper and enjoying Michael's expert cooking. He was so thrilled to have her home and in good health he overloaded their dinner plates with her favorite Italian dishes. That evening he was thinking about a shrimp dish. Jumping into the car he drove to the Asian market and purchased two pounds of prawns. True, his mind was not on the road when he had a collision with an oversized construction truck at the busy intersection one mile from his home. His car was totaled while the truck suffered a few scrapes. His vehicle went to the junk yard and he rented a sedan. Carrying the precious shrimp home, he created a gourmet meal, popped open an aged Cabernet and shortly after, the family fell sound asleep. The next morning, in the clarity of sunny skies, he could hardly get out of bed. Diane rushed him to the doctor who prescribed Lortab, a highly addictive pain killer.

Within a short period of time he became addicted. The drug did the trick killing the pain from the auto accident. When the prescription ran dry, the doctor merely refilled it, no questions asked. This inadvertent addiction would come back to haunt Michael.

Over a long meal at their home, Diane's parents came up with a great idea, one that would implement Michael and Diane's talents. A magazine. There was no local magazine that was centered on Las Vegas. A tourist town, perched on the edge of another building explosion the timing seemed in sync. Wouldn't it be great if they had a magazine that would inform the tourists about the entertainment, restaurants, shopping, the weather and special events? With Diane's talent as a graphic artist she could produce a creative magazine that jumped out at newsstands and with

Michael's sales talent and connections in the entertainment industry, he could provide valuable and insightful articles. It didn't take the couple more than a moment to commit to this new investment.

In 1999 Las Vegas Image was launched

The circulation began at 150,000 issues and it would be printed bi-monthly.

They rented a one-story office building off Flamingo and filled the six offices with writers, sales staff, photographers, a bookkeeper, outside consultants, printers and an editor. Using the finest heavy paper, the cover was sturdy and eye catching. As soon as the magazine was placed on the shelves it flew off. Michael found ideal locations and as fast as the shelves were stocked, the magazine was sold.

Michael's job was to procure advertisers, the most difficult task with a start-up magazine but when he laid out the interviews and those who would be advertising, the sponsors made room in their budgets. Interviewing superstars such as Jerry Lewis, Pat Cooper, Neil Sedaka, Smothers Brothers, The Righteous Brothers, Paul Anka, and Billy Davis, convinced potential advertisers that the magazine would succeed. Michael would call the star and meet them in their home or do a phone interview. A talker and an even better listener, the interviews became famous and a big part of the magazine. Tourists arrived in the city to see the stars they had read about and frequented the casinos where those stars were preforming. The Orleans was the first major casino to purchase a full-page ad. It all paid off, tourists were enticed to see the performers they had read about. They bought tickets to the shows and lingered afterward turning to the tables and slot machines for additional entertainment. It was a win- win for everyone.

Selling timeshares had taught Michael about the importance of getting your foot in the door; you had to get noticed. One of his tactics was to purchase tickets to a show and give them to perspective sponsors. "Just listen to me for five minutes," said Michael, "and I will give you two tickets to *Legends in Concert*."

That tactic got him into the door and once inside, *no*, wasn't in Michael's mind. Within three months the magazine's sales skyrocketed and he was able to place the periodical on newsstands in eleven states and numerous large cities, including Manhattan, Atlantic City, Dallas, Salt Lake City and Hollywood. Diane and Michael were working constantly but they absolutely loved the business. Each implemented their unique talents to the upmost which became rewarding and successful.

Michael often invited the performing artists to his home for dinner and they gladly appeared, his fame at cooking was a very big part of his persona. After a glass of wine and a spectacular homecooked meal, the famous entertainers were putty in Michael's hands. They talked freely and openly and when the interviews were completed, Michael unearthed secrets that piqued the readers' interest.

The circulation continued to grow. After reviewing one issue the reader was hooked, no one wrote about the performers the way Michael did. He was careful and was never malicious, yet he was always candid. The magazine garnered respect and performers wanted to be included in the magazine. It was a concentric circle of success that was growing at geometric progressions. Within three months they had a staff of thirty employees.

Michael knew how to organize a company and every Monday morning, he held an all staff meeting where he planned the week, set goals, listed the articles to be published and interacted with the staff. Anyone who had an idea was respectfully listened to. Sometimes people laughed, but he would say there is no such thing as a bad idea, just bad intentions.

The magazine hummed like a well-oiled machine and Diane's parents were quite satisfied with the results; they were turning a profit. Although the magazine was known for its star interviews, it was eclectic and included a section for book reviews, articles by medical doctors, restaurant reviews, recipes by Michael, a financial page, a calendar of events, beauty tips and new consumer products, things to do with young families, travel tips, a teen page, a page devoted to pets, a map of the city, and editorials. The broad spectrum of articles appealed to a broad spectrum of readers. It was a magazine that could be shared with people of all ages, from young kids to octogenarians. The bond paper used was sturdy enough to last through several readers. All the right variables came together to form a successful magazine.

Rebecca was one of the editors, her job was to produce the fashion page, highlighting designer woman's clothing available in the city, an enviable position. She did it well. When she took the position at *Las Vegas Image*, she requested a job for her young teenage daughter, Chelsea. Michael hired them both. Chelsea would write the teen page and assist the bookkeeper with payroll. As time progressed, she began to babysit young Elaina. Diane was happy, working on the magazine the hours were sometimes unpredictable and it was convenient to have a built-in babysitter. Elaina seemed to like Chelsea, and the situation was comfortable.

Rebecca had been living in the city a while and knew a lot of people. The Shaolin Monks, a famous performing group from China, wanted to test the waters in America and they asked her if she would be able to book their act in Las Vegas. She replied that she knew just the right person who could do that, Michael Leonetti. The group flew from China, arrived in Las Vegas and met Michael at his home.

He cooked dinner, offered drinks and they talked about the possibility of performing in Las Vegas. Their thinking was that people from around the globe visited the city and the unique performers would have an audience. Their kind of act had never been booked, it was chancy, it might go over really big or bomb. What they wanted from Michael was not only to book the act but produce the show, Las Vegas style.

Michael found a place to practice and they began putting the show together. He would produce it, tape it and then present it to the casinos. Using the group's basic performance art, he added women, upgraded the costumes, modernized the music, and created drama. When it was completed, it resembled the first type of Cirque du Soleil. There were one-hundred-thirty performers, plus musicians, stage hands and lighting and filming staff. It was a huge undertaking.

The project stole a lot of time away from the running the magazine, but Rebecca convinced him he would make a lot of money on the unique venture. Michael asked the group for money upfront, instead it was agreed he would receive a percentage of the ticket sales. At the end of the practices, the group went home to China and Michael began the arduous process of slicing and splicing a demo video he would use to sell to the entertainment directors. Cinevision was the sponsor and asked Michael to meet the executives in Vienna.

With hundreds of hours of tape from the practice sessions, he flew to Vienna and met with the sponsor. Presenting the sponsor with several hours of tape, he was asked to cull down the presentation to an hour or less. It was deemed excellent, the sponsor wanted to go ahead with producing the show. Las Vegas would be the first stop if Michael could get the entertainment directors to acquiesce.

After one week in Vienna, they shook hands and Michael returned to Las Vegas to sell the show. He had not received any money for his work, the sponsor believed the ticket sales would be extraordinary and more than compensate him for his work.

Diane picked him up at the airport. "Honey, you look exhausted," she said. "This thing is taking a lot of time away from the magazine, I hope it is worth it."

"Me too," he agreed, "I'm anxious and haven't earned a dime for all the work I have put into this. Cinevision, the sponsor, believes in the project and thinks I will earn a ton of money on my percentage of the ticket sales. I guess we will see. One thing for sure, there is nothing like this on the strip. It could be a huge draw but in the back of my mind, I have some reservations."

After a leisurely rest and a good meal, he returned to the magazine the following morning. The staff was busy and money was flowing in consistency from the advertisers. He made the time, picked up the phone and began canvassing the entertainment directors at the most prestigious casinos. He met with a few directors but it was MGM who picked up the show for a four-week residency.

The casino spent a substantial amount of money advertising the performance, flying in the troop and preparing the showroom.

He was excited when the performers arrived a chance to show the world a completely new form of entertainment. He orchestrated the production, set the rehearsals, the music, lighting and costumes. The casino collected the ticket money and marketed the show.

Opening night Michael dressed in a black suit and Diane in a long gown. It was the premiere and they wanted to look the part. They sat at the back of the theatre so they could view the show and observe the audience's reaction. The sold-out audience applauded and seemed to enjoy the show. When it was over there was little chatter as the audience departed, not a great sign. The first week, the show was sold out but as the weeks progressed, fewer and fewer tickets were purchased. The casino ended up giving away hundreds of tickets as comps to the high rollers. In one simple word it was a flop. Michael's take from the ticket sales was so little that he was disgusted and hired attorney Paul Scofield, to file a law suit against the Shaolin Monks. The Monks refused to meet with Michael, he needed a strong arm to get his payment. *They were not honorable.*

After consulting with his attorney, it seemed a futile effort to obtain his share of the profits. The troop hastily returned to China and refused to meet with Michael or his attorney. Angry, he felt used and abused.

The following morning, he called Rebecca into his office to discuss the situation. He was beyond mad. Rebecca had arranged the entire situation and held some accountability. In simple terms, Michael explained to Rebecca that he had been screwed. She was the one who set up this entire scenario.

"You made me believe you," Michael said in a low calm voice.

"I'm sorry the show wasn't popular. I guess we took a chance and it failed," she admitted.

"No, it was ME who took the chance, who spent time and money and received NOTHING! It is I who LOST! I am disgusted. You set me up and you screwed me!" he yelled.

"I had no intentions of hurting you. I thought this was

going to be great." I am done with you. Please get your stuff and leave," he shouted.

"Can you spare my daughter? She is an innocent pawn in this mess. She didn't do anything wrong. She loves working here and taking care of Elaina," cried Rebecca.

"Okay, Chelsea can stay," said Michael.

Rebecca quickly exited his office, went to her cubicle and assembled her personal affects in the quintessential brown box. She found her daughter and explained what occurred. "Do you want to stay here and work?"

"Sure mom. I love it here and I like Michael a lot, I want to stay." Rebecca kissed Chelsea good bye and left the company with her brown box.

It was a small office. Everyone overheard the yelling and observed Rebecca depart. For the balance of the day, the employees avoided Michael, he needed some time to cool down.

Later in the day, Chelsea came into his office. Perhaps she was checking the temperature on her position. Bringing in an article, she grabbed his arm, trying to get his attention, and presented her work. He smiled read the piece and told her to give it to the editor for final review.

"I hope you are not mad at me because I like you a lot." Michael shook his head and she began to leave the office. She turned and waited, she hoped he would say or do something but he kept his head down and ignored her.

Chapter 11

LIFE AT THE MAGAZINE CONTINUES

The Saturday night parties continued at Michael and Diane's home with at least one famous star appearing for dinner. All kinds of people arrived besides stars, there were doctors, lawyers, judges, congressmen and neighbors. Michael's arms reached out to everyone because everyone was a potential advertiser in the magazine. Not only did he offer a great meal and entertainment, but Michael would sit down with the guest and explain along with a beautifully placed ad, they could write an editorial. That perk was extremely effective. A plastic surgeon could place an ad but also be allowed several columns to write about their work and what they offered. That was how Michael sold hundreds of pages of advertising and how the magazine became eclectic and interesting.

At their parties, Diane took over the job as bartender since Michael was always in charge of the kitchen. In the corner of the living room, they built a bar and stocked it with prime liquor and bottles of wine. She purchased beautiful glassware and utensils, and carved fruit into artful pieces setting it on top of the drinks. There were fifteen guests for dinner that evening along with Diane's parents. They were enjoying a cocktail hour filled with fancy drinks and a bevy of cold appetizers. Michael sat at the piano and sang a few songs. He was smiling and everyone was having a joyful time. Great food, great music and a great group of people. Diane and Michael knew how to invite people who would interact with each other, they became gracious successful hostesses. When one was invited to their home, no one turned down the invitation.

After the entrée was served, Diane's father pulled Michael aside, "Can we chat?" They walked to the backyard where it was quiet and no one could disturb them. "Michael there is something weighing on my mind," Diane's dad began, "This Chelsea, I believe she is trouble and that you should have probably fired her when you fired Rebecca. You know I never butt into your running of the magazine. Son, I am very proud of what you have done and the success. This is a thorn in my side. I don't trust her. I think she has something up her sleeve.

Maybe I am an old fool or this is a premunition, but she strikes me as someone who might hurt you." "Dad, I can kind of understand why you say that. I caught her staring at me when I walk by. She has touched me more than once but I ignored it. She seems to have a crush on her boss and that is very common," said Michael. They walked back to the party with those warnings clinging in Michael's mind.

Dessert was served; a fruit gateau, a chocolate layer cake and a bowl of crème anglaise, with a collection of cordials, and espresso. It was after one in the morning when the last guest parted. Diane looked at Michael, "The dishes can wait until the morning."

Chelsea, the nightmare begins

Chelsea was happy at the magazine and thankful for the opportunity to write one of the pages each month; the teen page. That was a lot of responsibility for a young girl and she took the job seriously. It made the bookkeeping portion of her position palatable. For her age, she was drawing a nice salary and had few expenses. Her mother taught her well and she saved most of her earnings for college. Chelsea had many friends and one evening she received a desperate call from a girlfriend who confidentially told Chelsea she was pregnant and was planning to get an abortion but she needed $700.00, a lot of money for a teenager in high school. Chelsea had the money and was willing to give it to her friend based upon her commitment to repay the loan.

She went to the bank, withdrew the money in cash, met her friend the following day and handed over an envelope. Her friend was in tears and swore she would repay Chelsea as soon as she was able. But her girlfriend never repaid the loan. She kept on promising to pay but when it came time she offered excuse after excuse. The loan was never repaid. Chelsea was angry and confronted the girlfriend. They had a huge fight, both yelling at each other. Chelsea was sad that she had lost a friend over a loan, she had been the one who went out of her way to save her friend and was repaid with lies and deceit.

The girlfriend wanted to get back at Chelsea and what better way than destroying her position at the magazine. She was jealous of Chelsea's success. Hatching an evil plan, the girlfriend called the police and ranted that Chelsea was having an affair with Mr. Leonetti. That would guarantee that Chelsea would lose her job. Revenge would be served. When the complaint was filed with the police, they came to the home of Rebecca and Chelsea.

The police questioned the family and they were quite shocked at the allegations, vehemently denying anything happened between Chelsea and Mr. Leonetti. Later, the family signed a No Prosecution document clause dismissing any and all claims against Michael Leonetti. The entire situation was based on an immature teenager who sought revenge in the most evil manner. Nothing was ever done to the girlfriend. She was unscathed for all her lies and false accusations.

Michael had no choice, he hired an attorney to handle the matter. "And the police were flatly informed in unmistakable terms that there was absolutely no truth to it," stated Attorney Michael Root in his demand letter to the Las Vegas Metro on July 25, 2000. "Additionally, The Leonettis were flatly informed in unmistakable terms that there was absolutely no truth to it. The Leonettis later discovered that the likely source of this outrageous slander was an emotionally disturbed teenage girl who was jealous of Chelsea."

In mid-week Michael arrived home later than usual. Diane and Elaina were sitting in Elaina's room and she was crying. "Michael, I have to tell you something. Our daughter said that when Chelsea was babysitting her last weekend, Chelsea pulled out her breasts and rubbed her nipples with ice to show our eleven-year old daughter what happens. Elaina is very upset and doesn't want her babysitting again." After the initial shock sunk in, Michael became disgusted. The very next morning, Michael called Chelsea into his office and fired her for indecent exposure. "I trusted you with my daughter and that is how you behave! Please leave immediately." Michael thought back to the conversation with his father-in-law, he was right. He sensed this young girl was trouble. Michael was mad at himself that he hadn't fired her along with her mother. It was too late, the damage was done and his young daughter was traumatized.

"On March 24, 2000, Detective Jensen appeared in Mr. Leonetti's business office and without an arrest warrant arrested Mr. Leonetti in front of his wife, Diane, his daughter Elaina and their staff. Also in the office was a man who was negotiating to advertise in the Leonetti magazine and the magazine's photographer and his wife. Detective Jensen stated the grounds for arrest was that Mr. Leonetti failed to register as a felony sex offender. At the point of arrest, Mr.

and Mrs. Leonetti attempted to convince Detective Jensen that he was never convicted of either a felony or a sexual offense. Jensen's statement to the Leonettis was that he had been verbally told by the Lake Havasu Arizona Police that Mr. Leonetti was a felony sexual offender and that Detective Jensen, who had no documents of any kind stated, 'I don't need any paperwork. I have my facts straight.'"

Michael intended to fight fire with fire

He owned a magazine with a wide circulation and threatened to use it by putting the face of the Las Vegas Police officer on the front cover for false arrest. The detective rushed back to his office and relayed this message to the higher ups. The police force could not stand to be degraded in front of hundreds of thousands of readers in eleven states. Something had to be done to squash Michael's threat and get him out of the way for good. They weren't interested in following the rules of law, just in saving face.

Michael spent twenty-eight eternal hours in a holding tank at the Las Vegas city jail. After the guards patted him down for weapons, they confiscated his belt, his shoes, his wallet and the contents of his pockets. Walking him down the noisy hallway, the guard opened the cell door and forced Michael to enter. The new inmate shared the space with sixty other unlucky men. The temperature was cold as were the greetings he received from the other inmates.

When meal time arrived, it was a lone bologna sandwich wrapped in a paper towel. Hell was the proper description of the holding tank. With so many bodies in such a small space, he was on high alert every moment, sleep was an impossibility. The stink, the odor of unwashed bodies, the smell of feces and urine was so repugnant, he found himself gagging. For fear of reprisal, he held back, forcing himself to conceal any signs of weakness. The call from the corrections officer announcing he had made bail, undid his stupor. Escorted back to the front desk, Michael collected his personal affects, kissed his wife and they quickly drove home.

"Don't even say it, I know I stink," he said. "First a shower and then we will sit and discuss this craziness."

The bail was three hundred dollars," Diane mentioned, "Guess the Judge didn't think you are much of a flight risk. Between your family, and the business, the Judge explained you had too much to lose, so you got off cheaply. I must tell you that I would have arrived a lot sooner had I not been involved in a traffic accident. I was in such a hurry to get you out of jail that my mind was only focused on getting you out of jail."

Diane brewed a pot of coffee, cooked a ham and cheese omelet, and toasted several slices of Italian bread. Michael took a leisurely shower scrubbing himself from head to toe, dressed in clean clothing and joined Diane at the table.

After gobbling down the coffee and food, they began to discuss the hideous turn of events. With plenty of time in the holding cell, Michael reflected on what had caused the situation to arise, not once but twice in his life. He wondered how the arrest could have taken place. In Arizona, Michael was convicted of a misdemeanor of aggravated assault. No mention was ever made of sexual harassment or the use of the word felony. His offense was clearly at the very bottom rung of legal misdemeanor. His record was obtained from the Las Vegas Metropolitan Police records section on March 27, 2000 and was freely available to every officer including Detective Jensen at the time of Michael's arrest. Mulling over the detective's rationale, Michael couldn't rationalize the false arrest.

Clearly, splashing the false arrest on the cover of his magazine would exonerate him. "Diane, was there anything on the news about my false arrest?" asked Michael.

"That is strange, but good. In fact, nothing was mentioned in any media about your arrest. Don't you think it odd? One of the most famous people in our town was arrested and it was completely ignored by the media. Someone, or a lot of someones, are keeping this hushed up. Maybe the police fear you carrying out your threat, they don't want to see the face of an officer on the cover of a nationally distributed magazine, pointing out a gross mistake. I guess all of this will just go away." suggested Diane.

A letter dated May 19, 2000, from the State of Nevada, Department of Motor Vehicles and Public Safety, Division of Parole and Probation wrote as follows:

"Dear Mr. Michael Leonetti Biondo,
After reviewing information contained within your file, it is found that your conviction does not meet the registration requirements set for per the mandates of N.R.S. 179D. Therefore, this Division will be closing out our record and destroying your file."

A blatant fact that Michael's misdemeanor was just that and nothing more. He was a pillar of the Las Vegas community, his life exemplary. He was loved and respected not only by thousands who watched him perform but the local community.

Michael A. Root and James Guesman, served as Michael's attorneys. Known for specializing in divorce, they drafted a lengthy demand letter to the Southern Desert Correctional Center followed by a $250,000 lawsuit for false imprisonment. In the original demand letter Attorney Root stated: "…the facts evidence that Mr. Leonetti, without any cause, was unjustly and falsely arrested by Detective Jensen, an employee of the Las Vegas Metropolitan Police, which is a political subdivision of the State of Nevada. Because Detective Jensen failed to investigate or heed the nature of Mr. Leonetti's prior minor conviction, or obtain copies thereof, he was at least grossly negligent and at worst malicious when he arrested Mr. Leonetti. It is interesting to note that even a cursory look at Mr. Leonetti's LVMP record sheet evidences that Mr. Leonetti was not required to register in Nevada.

Because there was no probable cause nor arrest warrant for Mr. Leonetti's arrest this was a violation of 42 USC 1983, as it was a 4th and 14th

Constitutional Rights violation of Mr. Leonetti's right to be free from unreasonable search and seizure. In addition, Detective Jensen's failure to investigate, to obtain an arrest warrant, indifference to the Leonetti's claims, and his statements to the Leonetti's and others during and after the arrest, support an intentional disregard or intentional dislike for Mr. Leonetti and an intention to jail him for NO cause. To state the matter bluntly, the Leonettis believe, and the facts evidence that Detective Jensen with full knowledge of the minor nature of Mr. Leonetti's prior misdemeanor conviction, intentionally jailed Mr. Leonetti because he did not like him. To jail a man for no reason is the quintessential violation of 42 USC 1983".

In the demand letter, Attorneys Michael Root and James Guseman write, "Even a cursory glance at Mr. Leonetti's record sheet would have revealed that no probable cause existed to arrest him. We have also been advised that standard police procedure prior to an arrest of this type is to obtain hard copies of any prior conviction of the suspect. The failure to do so was an unexplained deviation from standard police procedure.

Stepping back, Michael reviewed the rational and couldn't comprehend where Detective Jensen's hate came from, nor how he had the ability to be a one man show in arresting an innocent man.

Chapter 12

Detective Jensen was angry that Michael's bail was easily paid and he was released in a day. The Detective's hard work in the false arrest was quickly undone. He loathed Michael and was jealous of his talent, his lifestyle, and his vast array of friends. His goal was to put Michael away for as long as the law allowed. He would show that performer who was the macho man, who had more power in the city.

The Detective began interviewing Chelsea and Rebecca. True, both woman had freely signed and admitted that no sexual activity of any kind had taken place but he thought if he dug harder, deeper and longer, he would persuade them to change their minds.

He met with Chelsea and her mother and casually discussed the situation and explained that it was possible to change their minds. Signed documents could be later reversed. If they were unhappy, he had the power to alter the course of Mr. Leonetti's life.

After another lengthy conversation with the mother and daughter, Detective Jensen was confident he was slowly changing their decision to sign the papers exonerating their boss.

Detective Jensen was obsessed with getting Michael. He approached him and insisted he take a lie detector exam. Michael denied the invitation on no uncertain terms and told Jensen not to bother him again. If he wanted anything, he was to contact Michael's attorney, James Guesman. "Leave me alone," screamed Michael. "Get out of my office and get out of my life. Don't you have other real guilty people to go after? What is your problem? Mad you couldn't make your allegations against me stick? Get the hell out of here! Don't ever show your face to me again! You and I both know those allegations were made up and I have a copy of their confessions to prove it!" ranted Michael.

The next morning Michael and his attorney went to the records department of Las Vegas Metro to obtain copies of any and all records filed under Michael Leonetti. There were no documents of any sexual assault charges, there were no records of any kind that would serve as cause for Detective Jensen to arrest Michael. There was never any reason for the false arrest. Detective Jensen was a person, he had biases but he was not a judge nor a jury. Whatever his obsession with destroying Michael's life, it could not be found in any court actions, there simply wasn't any illegal behavior. Hating a person was not grounds for putting him in jail. Stalking Michael, and Rebecca and Chelsea didn't uncover any wrongdoing. The detective had become a man obsessed with destroying Michael Leonetti.

"Satisfied?" asked Attorney Guesman. "This Detective has nothing on you. Look, I can't explain his problem, why he is stalking you, why the absurd obsession but clearly there is nothing in the records that validate any of his allegations. Please go on with your life and if the Detective comes around again call me. Don't threaten him, don't talk to him. Call me. Understood? We have plenty of ammunition to file a false arrest law suit. You will win hands down. We have both reviewed the proof."

Michael held his breath, "Okay, I promise. But"

"There is no but, just call me," instructed Attorney Guesman. The two men departed, each returning to their respective offices.

As Michael's mind wound around the situation, regardless of his attorney's advice, he wanted revenge. The humiliation of the false arrest, thrown into the city jail, cuffed and arrested in front of his wife, advertisers and employees was too much for him to handle. Returning to the office, he contacted the District Attorney's office and requested to speak with David Rogers, head of the department. The secretary notified Rogers that the owner of *Las Vegas Image* was on the phone and wished to speak with him. Michael left a message. No conversation took place. The assistant simply jotted down a message.

"I have served the Demand Letter for false imprisonment," announced Attorney Guesman. "Let's sit back and see how they respond. They have twenty work week days to answer the allegations."

On July 26, 2000 the Las Vegas Police Department responded. Seven police officers barged into the magazine and arrested Michael for a sexual assault complaint against Chelsea. That time there was a warrant, that time there were three police cars and that time they meant business. That was no fishing expedition. They lowered Michael's head, put him in the back of the squad car and returned him to the city jail.

Hysterical, he screamed to Diane, "Call my attorney!" Hands trembling, she picked up the phone. Glimpsing out the window she witnessed her spouse arrested, cuffed and driven off to jail. Shortly thereafter, Attorney Guesman arrived in a solemn mood. "I warned you to let this all go but you didn't listen. This isn't good." End of conversation.

The scene was a fleeting moment. Michael was transported to the county jail where the officers forced him to surrender his street clothes for jail cell blues. His eyes were flashing, his hands trembling, he was shaking from the cold, yet he was sweating, fraught with anxiety and severely agitated. Attuned to his everyday routine he had ignored his addiction to Lortab. When he was whisked off to jail there wasn't a moment of hesitation, nor time to think. Seven police officers made sure of that. Pacing the cell, his symptoms grew worse until suicide was on his mind. Once a day the guards opened the cell doors and allowed the holdees an hour to walk around the communal yard. Michael saw a way to end his life. There was a ledge outside his cell. When the cell door clicked open he climbed on top of the ledge, spread his arms and dropped to the ground one story below. Several guards ran to his broken body, called for a gurney and carted him off to the local hospital. No one cared about his addiction, they weren't there to hold his hand and rehabilitate him. With a couple broken bones, and numerous bruises, the hospital released him back to the county jail a day later. He suffered and suffered until the withdrawal was finally over.

On October 16, 2000, Michael received his sentence of 2 - 20 years. On the same date, Diane arrived at Attorney Guesman's office. Dressed in black, she was about to put to death her twenty-five-marriage to Michael Leonetti. She was broken. Her parents had gently suggested, then cajoled and finally threatened. She signed the Divorce Decree which dictated sole custody of Elaina, the house, the car and the contents of the house. He would get nothing. The papers were filed with the District Court Family Division. It was ordered that Diane would have sole custody, that Michael would have no visitation rights due to being incarcerated for crimes related to a minor-aged child, he was to pay one-hundred dollars a month for child support until the child reached eighteen-years of age, the marital residence reverted to Diane, along with the 1991 Cadillac and the magazine.

When Michael saw his attorney he smiled, "I hope you brought me some good news. I'm going crazy in this place." Guesman said nothing. With a grimace, he pulled out a brown manila envelope, extracted a pen from his pocket and handed the package to his client. "What's this?

A Divorce Decree? Diane is divorcing me?" he yelled. "How can that be? She loves me and I love her and I love our child."

"She is divorcing you. Please sign. I brought a copy for you to review and from the looks of things you will have plenty of time to review all of the stipulations," advised Guesman.

Michael had little choice, he signed the decree. He was too angry to cry. He was numb. For once in his life, he had no retort. He was living a nightmare. The pain from the Lortab withdrawal seemed small in comparison. He was losing his family. *How could this be? How can Guesman represent both me and Diane, my wife, now my ex-wife? How could all of this happen in an instant? How could I have been shut out from what was going on? How can I ever trust Guesman again?*

Carrying the thin document back to his cell he threw it onto the cot and hid it under the pillow. The tears began to flow. Nothing made any sense. What had gone so terribly wrong? It what seemed like a nanosecond his life was gutted like a fish. He was left with nothing but bare bones. The tears never stopped flowing.

Chapter 13

What Michael did not know

Michael did know Diane's parents were wealthy and had given them financial support over the years, especially for the magazine. What he didn't know was that they did not like him and never felt he was good enough for their daughter. When Elaina arrived their feelings of loathing for him escalated. They hid their feelings well.

James Guseman, Michael's attorney, also represented Diane, Michael's spouse, a direct conflict of interest. Any paralegal knows in Family Law, that the plaintiff and the defendant must have separate representation. One attorney can't represent both sides, someone will not receive a rigorous defense and in this case, it was Michael.

James Guseman was involved in the purchase of real property that would be used to build a casino. The individuals the attorney represented were Diane's father, (Michael's father-in-law), and Rebecca, (Michael's ex-employee). It was in the attorney's direct interest to keep Michael at bay and out of the picture. Guseman was to receive one million dollars when the purchase came to fruition. Again, a direct and blatant conflict of interest. With Michael safely tucked away in prison, Guseman was satisfying the wants and needs of persons who were in conflict with Michael. Guesman stood to financially gain with the parties who were in direct conflict with Michael.

Stewing in the county jail, Michael ticked off every day until his trial. He would have his day in court, he would take the witness stand and he would tell the truth. He would be exonerated!

It was what Michael did not know that would be his undoing. He had no reason not to trust his attorney. Although the divorce was too much to bear, he had all the confidence in the world when it came to Guseman's defense; his astute lawyer would come to the rescue. Remembering when they researched the records together, the attorney gave all appearances that he supported Michael. What Michael didn't know was where the attorney's bread was being buttered and how much butter was involved.

A few days before the trial, Guseman appeared at the jail to consult with his client. Inside his briefcase were several legal pleadings, pens and a bottle of water. He arrived with one purpose in mind and that was to convince his client to take a plea deal. That would end the ordeal and both men could get on with their lives. Michael was brought to his attorney in handcuffs while they conversed through the ubiquitous glass windows. He wasn't smiling, he was anxious, soon he would get his chance to tell his story and get out of jail. Michael sensed a sour disposition on Guseman's stiff, emotionless face as he purposefully diverted his eyes away from his client. His attorney began by asking how he was getting along, keeping it caring and cordial and then redirected the conversation to the purpose of the visit. "I want you to consider taking the plea deal. I promise you at most you will get twelve months and then you will be out and a free man."

"I didn't do anything wrong. You and I both know that. How can you ask me to take a plea deal? I won't I can't!" Michael screamed.

"You ruffled too many feathers and the DA would like to see you stuck in jail for a long time. The Judge will give you a slap on your wrist and twelve months, tops," advised his attorney.

"Even one day in jail is one day too long when you are innocent and did nothing wrong. No! No! No! I can't take the deal!" he repeated. "Look, if you don't take this deal, I can make no guarantees what a trial will bring. Please consider signing this paper," urged Guseman. He leaned over extracted the pleading and a pen, pushed it through the portal and into his client's hands. "Just sign it." Michael was dripping with perspiration, his legs were shaking, and his hands quivering. With great trepidation, he scribbled his name at the very bottom of the plea deal. Guseman quickly grabbed the document, got up, and said, "See you in court."

Somberly walking back to his cell, he felt a shudder snake through his body, that very same feeling he had the day he prayed to Jesus to save Diane and take him instead.

Michael shuffled into the courtroom, dressed in the county jail uniform, shackled in chains. The judge wore an expressionless face as he ordered Michael and Guseman to stand for the sentencing; he ordered twenty years, the maximum penalty for attempted sexual assault. The entire hearing lasted fifteen minutes. Guseman was silent, never offering any kind of defense. Michael was so overwhelmed with the shocking sentence, he passed out. He never got his day in court. He never got his chance to state the truth. He had been duped, convinced that pleading guilty would translate into a short time in jail. Twisting around he looked into Diane's somber face. That would be the last time he would ever see her or his daughter. It was as if they vanished into thin air. Twenty-five years of sharing their lives together, wiped out in an instant.

The sentencing was over in a blink of any eye and two days later he was transported to High Desert Prison.

Michael's life had transformed into a living hell. It was what he did NOT know that was his undoing. His wife was gone, his daughter was gone, his business closed, his home vanished. When his attorney never batted an eye while the sentence was recited, Michael should have read between the lines. He did not know. He just didn't know.

Years passed as he served time in prison. Turning his head, he noticed the cook struggling with a large package of meat. He couldn't help himself, he blurted out, "If you twist the package around and use that other knife, you can get that open in a second." Rather than argue, the young kid listened and in fact the advice was correct. Soon after, that cook came to Michael for advice on every aspect of cooking but Michael would never give away the fact he was a great cook and a great chef. Others followed, and soon he was advising the staff of fifteen how to prepare the meager ingredients. Guards hear all and know all and Michael's reputation as a talented cook piqued their interest.

One afternoon as Michael was scrubbing one of dozens of pots, a guard approached him and asked if he would cook food for the guards and the warden. It wouldn't be the food given the prisoners, it would be real food purchased from a grocery store. Michael's quick response was that he would be happy to oblige on one condition; the kitchen staff, who would be assisting him, would also eat the food he prepared. The Guard agreed that he would allow this freedom once and then he would talk among the Warden and the other guards to see if they agreed on the arrangement. When the steak pizzaiola, smothered in marinara sauce, with fettucine alfredo, sautéed mushrooms, a fresh arugula salad, and Italian wedding cake, crossed over their taste buds, and into their stomachs, the answer was unanimous and instantaneous. Yes, the staff agreed to allow Michael to reign as the head chef and the kitchen staff would be allowed to eat the same food. There was one catch; no alcohol, an important ingredient in many dishes. Making special food for the guards and kitchen staff was already stretching the rules, Michael knew he couldn't press for much more. One day at a time, one meal at a time and he would hopefully survive this nightmare. Diversion was a good thing for Michael.

Stepping into the kitchen, he rounded up the staff and informed them what they would be cooking. He would then instruct them how to make the dishes, and how to properly serve the food. Food had to not only appeal to one's sense of smell but it also had to look good. He taught them how to garnish the plates and when the guards and Warden were handed dinner, each plate looked like it had emerged from a five-star restaurant. The kitchen staff was happy, for once, they were eating well, learning something new and allowed to be creative.

Michael chuckled to himself when he overheard the guys discussing different types of garnishes and ideas for plating. For a few fleeting moments, his mind was focused on something other than the four walls of his cell. He made a lot of friends in the kitchen, and the guards grew to respect his talent. *I showed those guys how to make ravioli, lasagna, pizza with fresh cheeses, chicken dishes, all kinds of pasta, sauces, eggplant, fresh salads and cakes. I explained how to create a balanced menu. Most of the prisoners didn't have a clue what healthy tasty eating was about. By the time I left this prison, I had turned fifteen guys from potato peelers into decent cooks.*

Chapter 14

Prison life: August 16, 2000 to March 12, 2012

Michael shared a cell with another guy, who nicknamed him Crying Mike. He always had tears in his eyes. *It was like I returned home to a burning home to discover my wife and daughter had perished in flames and then the police said I committed arson. Life became a living hell, an endless nightmare where I could never wake up. What put me over the edge was when my cellmate had seen me crying. 'You better get used to this, cause it will be eight years before you sit in front of the parole board.' Which set me in a further tither and anther river of tears flowing. That small cell, that tiny cloistered space, that was my home. I hyperventilated and passed out.*

Michael quickly learned that he could appeal his case, but he had just four weeks to file the Appeal of Innocence. There were numerous jailhouse lawyers, a euphemism for inmates who spent all their free time in the law library researching their cases. When they became aware of his true innocence, he acquired a gaggle of such quasi lawyers who were happy to enlighten him. Under the four-week time limit, he filed his very first pleading in the District Court of Las Vegas; it began, I Michael Leonetti appeal the conviction. I am innocent of all charges. The jailhouse lawyers told him he had to wait for the court to respond and then he would continue filing pleadings. *Until when?* "Until the state releases you from prison," was their joint answer.

That insane process would continue for seventeen years. The inhumanity of the court system was at its best when they sentenced an innocent man for an act he never committed.

Simultaneously, Michael began another legal battle with the Decree of Divorce. A cursory reading of the simple document brought venin to the nostrils of the well-read inmates. Nevada was, and still is, a shared community property state. While his lawyer, James E. Guseman drafted a decree that gave the entire estate to his wife, Diane, he did so ignoring the community property laws. Being in prison didn't stipulate that Michael lost all that he had worked for in the twenty-five-year marriage.

Half of the wealth was legally his, half the house, half the personal possessions and half of the family cars. The inmates encouraged him to fight the decree. They instructed him in the art of drafting pleadings to the Family Court.

Compassion had disappeared from Michael's life, all his interactions with humans were fraught with disdain, prejudice and even hatred. Yet shackled in a holding cell at Family Court arose one gentleman who addressed Michael with compassion. It was Friday and traditionally, Steve Rushfield, Lieutenant for the Security Administrator for Family Court, cooked a meal for the employees. S e a t e d by himself in chains in the holding cell, Michael's nose twitched when it caught the aroma of freshly grilled meats. It tortured his stomach as he remembered the taste of grilled hotdogs and burgers. Further, he observed several employees chatting and munching on the fresh lunch. *What he wouldn't give for a taste of real food.* Putting his head down, his stomach forced him to remember and then Michael sprouted a stream of tears. His self-imposed misery was distracted by the rattle of keys at the cell door.

Looking up, Steve, the Security Administrator, offered a smile, a hotdog and some candy. Handing the food to Michael, he said a few kind words and relocked the cell door. That brief moment of kindness was stored in Michael's heart. He never forgot the generosity Steve had offered, the memory was embedded in Michael's mind forever; it restored faith that humanity had not completely disintegrated.

There was a total of 13 hearings objecting to Michael's Divorce Decree. He arrives at Family Court dressed in prison attire and shuffled into the courtroom with shackles on his legs and hands. What should have been a simple ruling extended to 13 hearings. With each new pleading, Michael came closer to taking back what was rightfully his. That was the first tiny sign in his pathetic life that perhaps justice was lurking somewhere in the future. Maybe he should concentrate on living.

Because he had no money, he represented himself at the 13 hearings. It was prejudicial that he wasn't allowed to wear street clothing and that he was fitted with chains on his hands and ankles. Pretty hard to sway a judge when one looked like a hardened criminal, yet Judge Robert Gaston's attention was based upon the law. Michael's drafts were based upon State of Nevada Statutes 60B, Mistakes, Inadvertence, Excusable Neglect, Newly Discovered Evidence, and Fraud. Michael won his case based upon fraud. The Judge reviewed the law, not the way the petitioner was dressed. For once in this unending nightmare, Michael received justice at the hands of the law. The Family Court Judge reviewed the assets of the marriage; Diane had spent all the liquid assets. All that was left was Michael's child support obligations. In lieu of splitting no assets, the Judge forgave the $10,000 child support and called the case resolved.

Five years later and 13 Motions with Family Court, he was escorted back to his living hell at prison, at least he had one win to cling onto.

After reading and reviewing the Order the one word that stuck out was FRAUD. The Court recognized that Michael's pleas were valid and that he had been cheated. Five months later, Michael was transported from High Desert Prison to Lovelock Correctional Institution, over four hundred miles northeast of Las Vegas. A medium custody institution, its population was much smaller than High Desert, with less security and more treatment programs. It was in fact, the prison where the infamous O J Simpson was housed. Its emphasis was on retraining and altering unacceptable behavior into acceptable behavior. There was an extensive law library, a plethora of classes and a large outdoor yard for exercise. Michael was taken from the transport bus, ushered into the receiving atrium, stripped, and given a state issued uniform designed by a manufacturer, Hard Timin, specialists in leisure attire. Blue and 100% cotton, it was designed for comfort and movement. The prison was mostly inhabited with nonviolent types of crimes. The inmates didn't bother each other, or threaten each other, they kept to themselves and didn't instigate violent confrontations, they were there to serve their time and leave.

A large portion of the inmates were sexual predators, many incestual relationships ended up in this prison. *How do you raise a child, love the child and then sexually abuse that child? I never associated with those guys. I could never understand how they could do that. Destroy the very thing they loved.*

The guard walked Michael up a set of cement steps, extracted the key to the cell, opened the door and he observed his newest inmate enter the cell. Slamming the door tightly, the guard walked away leaving Michael to deal with his cellmate. Michael glanced over at the bunk, took one look at his cellmate, sat down on the toilet, lowered his head and cried. He cried and cried and when he was done, he looked at the floor, he had literally cried a puddle of tears. *Was that even possible?*

At Lovelock Prison, the prisoners were segregated, (they said it was for their own safety). Whites and Blacks lived separately. When Michael glared at the man lying on the lower bunk, it was clear he was Black. *Was he to perish on the very first night?* He was not prejudiced, it was the system that had crafted the rules and clearly this situation seemed to break the rules, someone wanted him dead.

Michael finally rose from the steel toilet.

"Man, that is a lot of tears. Pal, are you okay? I am Morrey." He extended his hand and although reticent, Michael took his hand and shook it. "So, what are you in for?"

Afraid to respond Michael remained silent.

"Are you afraid of me? If you don't want to tell me your story then I will tell you mine. I am a lawyer, not a jailhouse lawyer but a real lawyer who did something bad and here I am."

"You a real lawyer?" asked Michael, "Because my lawyer screwed me big time."

"Everyone says that, but most of the time, it just isn't true. When the appeals were done most of the time the inmate received a rigorous defense."

"Not in my case," answered Michael. He began his story and this time Morrey was completely silent. Two hours later he finished and commenced to cry. "Now you know why I cry all the time."

"I have to tell you that is some horrible story. You were royally screwed. Conspiracy, plain and simple. You have been taken on a ride. That lawyer of yours is the one who should be behind bars not you. Pal, how about I help you? What do you say?"

"Sure, but I have no money," said Michael. "I'll do it for nothing but there are some court fees that you will have to pay. First, I will help you but put some money in your bank account so you can fight your case and get you the hell out of jail. It's not like the Monopoly Board game where you get out of jail with a free card. It will cost."

Morrey got up and signaled for Michael to follow him around the prison. They walked to the cafeteria, ate dinner, returned to their cell and fell asleep. The next morning, they went to the law library and began the rigorous defense he should have had in the first place.

"We need to show the courts the inept defense your attorney provided and the outrageous conflict of interest he bore before, during and after the sentence was read. We have to discredit James Guseman. That will be a piece of cake with all that you have told me."

Morrey took Michael for a short tour around the library and discovered he was a quick study. While Michael was busy researching defending his case, Morrey was busy researching the defense offered by Michael's attorney. There were more than enough statutes to put that attorney behind bars. Morrey had plenty of time. To him it was an outrage than any inmate who didn't deserve to be in prison shouldn't fight his way out. He was motivated to get the lawyer who did this heinous act on an innocent man. Like a dog with a juicy steak bone, he wasn't going to let go until his cellmate walked out of prison.

Morrey assisted Michael in stringing together a series of pleadings that they hoped would garner the attention of the Courts and force the Judge to see the conspiracy. On February 27, 2001, they filed a first pleading: Motion Application for Leave to Proceed, (all documents sent to the court were in Michael Leonetti's name only).

This was followed by letters, Motion to Clarify, an Emergency Motion to extend time, Motion for Excess Pages, Motion to Compel, a Memorandum regarding Resignation of his former Judge, a Memorandum to the Attorney General, another Letter, Motion for Default, Affidavit Motion for Federal District Court to Seek Redress (for violations under 18 U.S.C. 241 and 242), several additional Letters, Motion re: conspiracy and on February 13, 2008 Notice of Motion and Motion for Default Judgment. All in all, Michael filed over one-hundred pleadings. He sent pleadings to the State Court, the District Court, the Court of Appeals, and the District Supreme Court.Finally, the Court replied with an Order Granting extending the time for filing motions and allowing the excess pages. Creedence: the court debunked all the motions but allowed him time and the ability to add additional pages to his motions. All other motions were ordered Denied. At least the Court was receiving his motions, mulling them over, cogitating and making allowances.

Copies of all court documents were mailed to the prison. Reading the word "Denied," didn't deter Michael from fighting. He would prove his innocence no matter how long it took. All he needed was enough money to continue drafting pleadings to the Courts. He certainly had the time and with Morrey steering him into the law books, enough knowledge to make it happen.

He continued filing Motions to the Court, with one major request: Motion for Relief from Judgment. Short and sweet, he requested the Court turnover the guilty plea and release him from prison. The response was due within twenty calendar days. He was hoping and praying there would be no response and thus no objections to his request from the opposition but on the very next day there was a Judgment dismissing the action and the request to leave prison was squashed. Just another hurdle, Michael and Morrey immediately filed an Appeal. He then added numerous letters to the docket proving his innocence, none of which prevailed in setting him free.

On July 15, 2008 he filed a Memorandum on Actual Innocence, and another for transcripts. The Court ruled and issued an Order Denying all his Motions. The Motions with the State Court of Nevada began on February 23, 2007 and ended on January 26, 2009.

Along with a voracious appetite for learning the law, Michael took classes in psychology. It opened his eyes and mind as to why people acted the way they did. He gained an understanding of human nature and it made him tolerant and more understanding. Yet nothing would ever explain the horrific treatment he received at the hands of James Guseman, behavior that put Michael in prison.

Although Michael had found some distractions, he was absorbed in self-pity and sheer misery. Every time he walked into the cell, Morrey would shout, "Hi pal."

Michael's eyes would well up and he would shed tears. He never stopped crying. For the first three months at the new prison he slept with all his clothes on in a fetal position. He wanted to crawl inside himself and hide. But he couldn't. He was forced to wake up each morning living in a tiny cell, living a nightmare, living a life he didn't deserve. One morning after breakfast, he walked into the chapel, kneeled and prayed to Jesus to allow him to die. *I was in so much pain I wanted to die. This pain I had was so deep, in the pit of my stomach, I couldn't face another day. Death was my only salvation. I had lost all hope in life. Trapped in prison I saw no way out but death.*

An inmate tapped him on the shoulder and introduced himself as the Chaplin. "I know who you are," he began. "I saw you perform in Las Vegas and you are so talented. I love your voice and the music you sing. I could use your help," he said. Michael's head was bowed, "There is nothing I can do for you."

"Yes there is, you can help me fill this chapel. No one ever comes here. I know I can help some of the men, but first I need to get them to walk through the door."

Michael's head remained bowed as he continued to say "No" to the Chaplin's request.

"How about writing a play based on stories in the bible?" Michael picked up his head, thanked the Chaplin for being kind and walked back to his cell. When he returned he told Morrey about the experience, "The Chaplin wants me to write a play. I wouldn't know where to begin."

Morrey walked to a shelf pulled out a bible and handed

it to Michael. "Read this, it will give you an idea or two." The following day Michael returned to the chapel which was empty save for the Chaplin.

"Have you thought about my idea about writing a play? I know with your talent it can be done and then I can finally fill these pews and give hope to some of the inmates."

Michael sat down, bowed his head and the tears flowed. The Chaplin was patient and stopped talking.

When Michael finally rose the Chaplin said, "Job, write a play on Job."

"I'll think about it," he responded. Returning to the cell, he opened the bible and found the scripture.

After reading the story he began to envision how it might be performed. Although he had never written a play, he discovered there were a lot of things he had learned to do. He had the talent, the time, the space and a purpose. Purchasing paper and pens at the commissary he began writing the play, a much-needed distraction.

After the play was completed, Michael walked around the yard and began collecting a group of men to act the nineteen roles. Each day from 11:00 am until 3:00 pm, the prisoners were allowed to walk freely in the yard. There were nine hundred men, and he was confident there would be plenty volunteers.

He then went to the library, pulled out tons of music and spliced together a two-hour soundtrack which would serve as the background music. He held rehearsals and the play was performed to a full audience inside the chapel. The Chaplin was happy that inmates finally found their way inside the chapel and might take a piece of God with them after the performance.

He went on to write sixty plays based on bible stories. He was inclusive and used the Koran, and the First Testament. For seven years, the inmates attended presentations, walking away a little better, touched by God's words and an insight into the higher moral values of the human core. No one in the history of prison life had ever accomplished what Michael had done. He offered hope to those who needed hope and showed thousands the light religion can shed on a human's soul. For many, they experienced what love meant. He never received any monetary compensation nor acknowledgment for his efforts.

Michael continued perusing the bible voraciously seeking the next great play to offer the prisoners, something that would give them hope, a sense of self-worth, a love for God and humankind. *I would read the bible and I felt the pain of the people depicted in the stories. I truly believed that God showed me the light and wanted me to write the plays. When I performed, I felt as if I touched the flesh of my audience but in these bible plays, I felt like I touched the spirit inside the men. For me, it was a higher level of performing.* His plays did as he had hoped they would do, bringing to those who experienced his words a sense of love and respect for humankind. He salvaged the best in a prison society filled with men who had committed various types of crimes. *If I didn't lose everything and everyone I loved, I would have never understood the characters in the Bible. I had to walk in their shoes to internalize their pain, suffering and their emptiness. Experiencing those emotions gave me a true insight when I taught the inmates the parts they had to act."* Everyone in the prison came to know the playwriter and they sought him out for emotional and spiritual strength.

When the holidays arrived, especially Christmas, Michael produced and performed shows. Obtaining instruments and musicians, he put on a truly entertaining show. He found a new audience for his voice but it wasn't one of his choosing. The holidays were emotionally the worst time of the year. Everyone reminisced about their lives, their childhood, and what they were missing. It was their family, the joy of the season, the wonder of loving others and being loved. Prison was never intended to be a happy place but the words embedded on the sign, Lovelock read "Correctional Institution."

To further enhance the misery of the population, the night guards decided they would further remind the inmates what they were missing. At two o'clock in the morning, they would play Christmas tunes on the loud speaker. It served to wake up the prisoners, making them depressed and homesick. It also served another purpose, each year several inmates were so severely depressed, they hung themselves in their cells. Torture takes many forms and the seemingly innocuous act of playing Christmas music did what the guards wanted it to do; made the prisoners so miserable that many went beyond the breaking point. Some were savvy enough to insert plugs in their ears but for so many others, they suffered and endured the inhumane torture. The Warden did nothing. Although the shows served as a distraction they never altered Michael's misery nor altered one moment of his goal of returning to society. Morrey instructed Michael on the mechanics of court life. He would draft a pleading and they would wait for a response. Once received, they would draft an answer to the response and this would continue, continue until the day that prison door would open and Michael would see the light of day as a free man. Until that day, he and Morrey relentlessly researched and drafted pleadings.

Warden Cheryl Foster witnessed the value of Michael's biblical plays and the joy of his Christmas performances. He was a famous performer with a great voice who had an uncanny ability to make music when he was provided with no accoutrements. She had no idea nor inclination as to what was in his mind, she only knew that she wanted him to continue performing and creating the Christmas shows.

It was an inadvertent walk by which caught Jimmy Allen's eye. The chapel was crowded with inmates. A white guy was standing in the center directing where the twenty or so, inmates should stand and what they should say and how they should act. Holding up a bunch of papers, he encouraged the men to deliver their lines with genuine passion. *Hmmm,* thought *Jimmy, I know that guy, he wrote and produced a bunch of plays from the bible and produced a bunch of Christmas shows. He knows how to sing and I guess he must know how to write plays.* In fact, Jimmy had attended many of the shows Michael produced.

Observing the rehearsal, he was convinced this white

guy could probably do a decent job writing a play for Black History month. After the actors emptied the chapel, Jimmy lumbered up to the white guy and introduced himself.

"I've seen your plays and heard you sing. You are really good. How about doing a play for us Black guys? February is Black History month and I think it would be great if you open the eyes of these guys and showed them what happened to us Blacks in America."

It took little convincing for Michael to acquiesce to Jimmy's wishes. Shaking hands, he agreed to write and produce the plays. Another challenge and another diversion to keep his mind off his nightmarish circumstance. Walking purposefully to the library, he began researching Black history. Taking copious notes, he collected enough information and wrote a play centered on Martin Luther King, the man and his great deeds. After writing the play, he reviewed it with Jimmy. The next day they canvassed the population milling around the exercise yard, gathering enough men to act the roles. With no money for production, Michael did his best to offer music and meager costumes, but it was the message that was the headliner. The words spoken by the actors, delivered with frankness, would hopefully stir the hearts of the audience.

Jimmy was in charge of promotion, his goal was to raise the men's interest enough to show up for the event. By mid-afternoon, the gym was filled with over a thousand inmates. The subject piqued the curiosity of the Warden and other staff members, who also arrived anticipating a unique experience. With little fanfare, the play was performed and the men clapped and whistled when the last word was uttered. Walking away from the ninety-minute production, they felt more like brethren than inmates. Truly, through Martin Luther King's words, Michael had written an inspiring production.

After the actors took their bows, Jimmy introduced the playwright. Michael, one of the few white faces in the crowd, stood and waved. Although he wrote and directed the play, the real hero in the presentation was Jimmy. He convinced the inmates to participate and when they took in the message, it evolved into a healing and a coming together of the races.

The healing continued as Michael went on to write additional plays. *Rosa Parks* was well received as was King's famous *I've Got a Dream Speech.* A story rarely alluded to in Black History is the *Garbage Truck* story. In the early fifties, the Black garbage collectors were not allowed into the office buildings. The garbage was placed in the alleyways.

On a rainy day, the men wanted to enter the building for shelter but were barred, so they jumped into the back of the garbage truck for protection from the downpour. The truck driver, unaware the men were in the back of the truck, turned on the crushing device and all four men were crushed to death. It was a hideous scene and it woke up America. Needless deaths because of needless bigotry. February was coming to a close and after weeks of studying Black history, Michael came up with a completely original play, *Heaven's Grocery Store.* Enlightened through the research offered at the library, the story was based upon dozens of inventions created by African Americans. It shined the light on brilliant ideas, boasting the conception that the Black intellect was, at the very least, equal to the white population. It was time to be pragmatic, look at a person for what was harbored in his heart and mind, not the color of his skin.

The final consensus was that the plays facilitated an understanding and tolerance of races, creating a liaison between all walks of life. It raised the embedded anchor of shortsightedness and allowed the men to move a little more freely between races. Michael never forgot Jimmy. Their friendship was sealed and continued throughout their years in the prison and later in life.

Wrapped up in the biblical stories, Michael had lost interest in entertainment for entertainment's sake. When he donated his talent to the prison, it would only be to serve God. He lost all interest in producing the Christmas shows that were frivolous and light-hearted.

The following year, Warden Foster asked Michael to come to her office to discuss the upcoming Christmas show. When he explained he no longer wanted to do the show, she was angry.

Who was this guy that he could tell me what he can and can not do? I am the warden and I will tell him what he must do, she thought.

Michael walked out of her office unaware the Warden was bristling with hate for his arrogant attitude. He didn't want to produce the Christmas show, he never considered that earth shattering but he never saw the turndown through Warden Foster's eyes and ego. Later that day she sent several guards to his cell. They threw him against the wall and pressed his face into it until he could barely breathe. They handed him a paper the Warden wanted him to sign. Releasing him, he was shocked at what he read. It was a guilty plea for disobeying an order from the Warden. If he signed the guilty plea he would face ninety days in solitary confinement but if he refused to sign the plea she would add another one-hundred twenty days to his incarnation at the prison. Michael was left with no choice, adding additional time to time for his innocence was absurd. He signed the guilty plea and was whisked off to the hole to endure his punishment.

 The hole was a tiny cell devoid of all sunlight. He saw no one, interacted with no one and faced nothing but darkness for ninety excruciating days. Every three days he was allowed a short shower and ten minutes in the yard at two o'clock in the morning. He survived by prayer, every waking moment was filled with intense asking God to get him through this ordeal. *Are you testing me? Do you want to make me believe in your will and your strength? Is this how you are giving me strength by testing my will to continue on? Why me God? Why did my life turn into hell on this earth? I need you now so please stay with me. Keep me company. Walk with me through my waking moments. Ease my physical pain, ease my mental pain. Stay with me, please, I beg you, stay with me until I am released from this hole.*

One morning a guard brought his breakfast, "Hey play man, here is your food." The guard spat into the breakfast and pushed it through the tiny aperture in the metal door. Michael took the food and placed in on the cell floor. He never touched it. Dogs were treated better, hell most living things were treated better than he. Michael's entire life. His total existence had turned into juxtaposition, here was an innocent man, a talented performer who had been constantly surrounded by loved ones, now he suffered alone with the most meager food and no creature comforts. The only comfort he had was his belief in God. His sanity and his heart were the two things the Warden could not take away.

When the ninety days passed, a guard arrived, jingled the keys, unlocked the cell door and guided him back to his old cell. A bit of sunlight hit his face and he squinted his eyes. He had adapted to total darkness and the sudden bright sunlight was harsh. Sheltering his eyes and he stumbled into his cell, climbed up to the top bunk, looked up at the ceiling and cried. He thanked God for keeping him alive and prayed he would make it through the day. A shower and palatable food slowly brightened his spirits. Later at mail call he was pleasantly surprised when he was handed a stack of letters from his mom. He immediately sat down and wrote her a series of letters, explaining the horror of solitary confinement and the absurd reason he was sent there.

He tried to put the ninety days of solitary hell behind him, blotting out the mental and physical pain, but that would prove to be impossible. If nothing else, he was humbled, appreciating the simplest things in life, a fresh piece of toast, water for bathing, and the beauty of sunlight. God had not forsaken him, God had provided Michael the strength he needed to fight for life. Returning to the open yard every inmate came over, shook his hand, slapped him on the back hugged him and told him how happy they were to see the return of the play man. Albert came over, sat down and talked. "You have given so much to the men in this place and look how the Warden treats you. There are three things that make a man worthy; the content of his character, compassion for others and integrity. You have all those. We all know that, we all know you are innocent." Albert slapped Michael on the back and walked away.

A concept never discussed among the prisoners (or most law-abiding citizens) was the business of prison. In fact, prison was (and still is) a thriving business; thousands of people work across America inside prison walls. Some states have gone so far as to privatize prisons, recognizing it was truly a lucrative enterprise. What made this business successful? It was the guarantee that the cells would be fully inhabited with a growing population. That was how the Warden, down to the lowest employee has maintained, their jobs. Thus, when the Warden doled out additional time for prisoners, whom the Warden deemed necessary, it served to further guarantee employment by insuring the inmate population. In prison, there was no jury of one's peers, it was only the Warden.

In Michael's situation he had no alternative other than

to accept the hideous punishment. It was her and her alone who decided the prisoner's fate; hardly justice, hardly the intention of the American constitution. Once trapped behind prison walls, all individual rights eviscerated, and what remained was a shell of a person, whose treatment was less than an ant creeping in the dirt. Humanity dissolved, life was ruled by the Warden ruling the kingdom (the prisoners). All mail going and coming was scrutinized, Word leaking of cruelty meant the conduit was punished either by time in the hole or inadvertently, death. The Warden had no sympathy for anyone leaking the truth or the overzealous cruel punishments. For Michael, the inhumane treatment could only be unfurled when he was released from the confines of hell. Until that moment happened, he would accept his fate and pray that God would keep him alive to see another day.

As a former attorney, Morrey, Michael's cellmate, held an extra grudge against James Guesman. Becoming an attorney, one must take an oath to abide by the law and to give all clients a rigorous and unbiased defense. Not only did his attorney not uphold the law, nor provide a rigorous defense, but through Morrey's eyes, he had plotted a conspiracy that would get Michael out of the picture and out of the way, permanently.

Prison life was as routinized as life could possibly get. The only two things that changed were the weather and the date on the calendar. Michael ate three meals a day, slept and prayed. Not a day went by that he didn't stop in the chapel and pray. The Chaplin developed a love for

Michael, he was in awe of his talents and his charisma. For the first time, the prisoners were coming to the chapel, some for formal services on Sunday mornings, some for bible classes and some entered at all hours to prayer. The once barren pews were now filled with men. The Chaplin had at last found an audience to receive his insights and commence the process of accepting God in their lives. For that the Chaplin would always be indebted to Michael for making that happen.

At mail call, Michael tore open the daily letter from his mother. It was the usual greeting and the usual unconditional expression of her undying love. She always had so much to say but mostly she wrote about Michael Jr, Michael's son, her grandson, the only one she would ever have. Joy, Michael's sister, never found love, never married and never had children. It was Michael Jr. who Dolores doted on day and night. She was very proud that in spite of his horrible illness making him disabled, he was able to become his own person.

Eventually he moved out of Dolores's home and rented a small apartment. He rarely dated and never married. The two were very close. She loved teaching him to cook and he in turn would show her how to fix simple things in the home. Folding the letter, he slipped it inside his pant pocket.

Chapter 15

A Conditional Guilty Plea

Morrey's tenacious court actions eventually came to fruition. The first draft uploaded to the District Court alleging James E, Guseman had a conflict of interest when he filed the Divorce Decree and later when he convinced Michael to take a plea, was answered by the Court with an emphatic "No."

As soon as the answer was read by Morrey and Michael, they filed the first response. With each new pleading, more details were illuminated on the original allegations. On May 30, 2001, The State Bar of Nevada Disciplinary Board filed a Public Reprimand regarding James E Guseman, Esq. Within the pleading was a plethora of other cases in addition to Michael's case, (five other cases cited). "You were counsel of record for Michael Leonetti in his guilty plea resulting in a criminal conviction (Leonetti v State 36980). During the course of an appeal, which was unknown to you at the time, you failed to respond to any of the notices and orders sent to you by the Supreme Court of Nevada. All written communication to you was returned to the Court.

On March 26, 2001, the Supreme Court entered an order, which was served on you, remanding the case to the District Court to secure new appellate counsel. In light of the forgoing, the designated hearing panel found that you violated SCR 79 and SCR 173(3) (Knowingly disobeying an obligation under the rules of a tribunal). Pursuant to the terms of your conditional guilty plea agreement, you are also hereby placed on probation for a period of two years with conditions set forth in the Conditional Guilty Plea."

Unscathed, for all intense and purposes, James E Guseman walked away with a slap on his wrists while his client, Michael, rotted away in prison. There was nothing in the pleading about remorse, nor was it apologetic. He didn't lose his license to practice law, nor suffer any financial loss. He remained intact, nothing lost, nothing gained.

The recognition that James E Guseman had done a bad thing, in fact many bad things in Michael's case should have sent a tsunami to other attorneys standing in line to assist an innocent man out of prison, but it didn't. Case in point, Roberto Miranda, had sat on Death Row for fourteen years and was released based upon another attorney believing in his innocence. Not so in this case.

It would be five years before Michael filed an official complaint and when James E Gusman was found guilty, it should had been an expeditious step to Michael's release from prison but it wasn't. All the proof he needed of his innocence was readily apparent in Guseman's Conditional Guilty plea but apparently the Courts didn't translate it that way. It was another four years before Michael would get his day in court for an evidentiary hearing. There was NO evidence that Michael ever committed a crime yet his own attorney was guilty of a plethora of charges regarding Michael's case. Guseman never went to jail but Michael was sent to jail. That hearing was a redundant exposure of Guseman's illegal and unethical behavior. Guseman was angry he had to face Michael in a courtroom. The Judge called for a break and Guseman, along with Diane, and Diane's father (Michael's ex-father-in-law), walked out of the courtroom and huddled in the hallway. A conversation ensued that the three never realized was being recorded in the ears of two people who overheard their discussion.

Diane's father, "I'm tired of the shit Michael is putting us through."

Guseman, "I can have him taken care of in prison."

Diane's father, "I'll pay whatever it takes to have him killed."

The two witnesses privy to this conversation were Bob Knighten and his daughter Christina, who happened to be in the hallway standing in close proximity to the three people huddled together. The two witnesses went back into the courtroom and told the Bailiff what they had just overheard. The Bailiff turned to the Judge and relayed the conversation overheard by the two witnesses. The Judge didn't act upon the notice, in her eyes, it was here say. The hearing ended quickly and Michael shuffled out of the courtroom and was transported back to the prison. A slam of the heavy wooden gavel and he lost the first round. No reprieve, no get out of jail. He was remanded back to hell.

How did Michael learn about the conversation which took place between his ex-lawyer, ex-wife and ex-father-in-law? He remained in the courtroom while it was taking place. It was a letter he received in prison from Bob Knighton and Christina Knighton. Michael went ballistic when he found out of the conspiracy. What began as an Evidentiary Hearing morphed into a conspiracy and an imminent fear he was about to be murdered. The three individuals had the motive, the means and the ability to have Michael murdered. Michael was crazier than crazy.

He was a sitting duck! What to do! Who would listen to this plot? He knew the Warden would brush it off as just another prisoner complaining. He couldn't call the local newspapers or radio stations. He didn't have the Internet at his disposal to broadcast the conspiracy. He was trapped, stewing in jail just waiting for a bullet to enter his head, or a sucker punch to his heart. He had to figure out a way which would let the world know of this plan. The answer came to him: The Court system. If he drafted a letter to the Court, it would be a permanent record of what had transpired. It was as if he were dropping bread crumbs leading investigators to the plotters of his life. His death would easily be solved by simply reviewing the Court records and reading the names of those who plotted Michael's fate. Ironically, it was the Court that put him in jail, but upon his death (if it should occur behind bars) it would be the Court that revealed his killers. Back in his cell, he and his cellmate drafted a series of pleadings implementing Federal Law 18 USC subsection 4, ",,, anytime an officer of the court is notified a crime is being committed they are compelled to notify authorities. Failure to do so is three years in prison." He wrote back to Bob and Christina Knighton thanking them for the information and requesting they add at the bottom the following sentence, "signed with the understanding of perjury" and that the affidavits be notarized. Several days later, the two witnesses returned the letters with the additional clause added and notarized. That was proof that Michael's conspiracy theory was a lot more than just a theory, he held the proof in his hands. Three people wanted him dead. He was out of their way, yet even in prison he was causing havoc with their lives. Death would be the only way to shut him up.

Once he held the evidence needed, Michael tried to prove his case by subpoenaing the Bailiff who was on duty the day of the hearing. When he requested the records, the Court responded they did not keep records of the name of the bailiff and would not release that information. It would appear a dead end for Michael. He knew better, as did his jailhouse lawyers. The employees were paid by the state and every minute they are on the clock was recorded. There were documents, but they would never be released to Michael.

MICHAEL LEONETTI

A LETTER ASKING FOR FREEDOM

Compelling, it should have done what it intended it to do and free an innocent man. It was written to a seasoned and respected judge. The letter was meant to get Michael out of jail. He feared for his life. He needed to force someone to listen and believe his fate. As Michael saw it, the only person on earth who could save his life 3was the Judge. He had no alternatives and no one who had the power to stop his death from happening. Desperate, he clung to the only option available, the only public forum that would air the conspiracy.

It began: *RE: Resignation form the bench and to turn yourself in to the proper authorities.*

Dear Judge,

You were assigned this case on January 8, 2004, you went against the Orders of the Supreme Court's August 20, 2002 Order of Reversal and remand case No. 39531. You refused to hear the May 9, 2001 Habeas Corpus Petition Appellant's May 9, 2001 Motion to Withdraw the Guilty Plea and all of the subsequent documents filed by appellant in effort to litigate his petition and Motion.

You have done all you can to sweep under the rug the criminal conduct that was done to me by the State of Nevada in my case to protect and hide the false arrest that was done to me by the Las Vegas Police Dept. in March of 2000. You knew all along that James E. Guseman was Guilty but your choice was to cover-up for Guseman and the State. You knew that the victim signed a Police Report that she was never assaulted in anyway by me, however three months later as soon as she was fired from my magazine for sexually assaulting my eleven-year-old daughter, she changed her story, and points the finger at me.

There was No Probable Cause to arrest me. However, this was the Perfect Opportunity to cover up the $250,000 claim that was being filed against the Las Vegas Police Dept. and the fear of being put on the front cover of my next issue.

On April 2, 2004 at the hearing you were told by your Bailiff that James E. Guseman was conspiring to have me MURDERED in prison or when I get out, you instructed your Bailiff NOT; to report the crime, you both had a duty, but you failed and committed a Class B Felony. Guseman had all the motive to carry out his plan. Once again you covered up for Guseman. You knew that Guseman signed a Guilty Plea May 1, 2001, you knew that Guseman was a psychopath. Guseman defrauded myself and five other victims, you knew and Leon Simion knew that Guesman was lying under oath and was not telling the truth, the evidence was right in front of you both, but you kept quiet. There is enough evidence against you to take to the Grand Jury for an Indictment, your unconsciousable actions has put the District Attorney, Attorney General, Nevada Bar and the Judicial Disciplinary Commission in a very Embarrassing Situation, your deliberate Disobedience has jeopardized the integrity of those that are there to enforce the law.

A Judge is disqualified whenever the Judge's impartiality might reasonably be questioned. There is enough evidence under Federal Law 42 U.S.C. to put you in a prison for ten years. For the sake of Justice and for the people that voted you in office step down from the bench and get the proper help you need. You have been accused of breaking the law, now it is your turn to stand for what is right. When you speak the Truth, you declare Righteousness. As Supreme Court Justice Rose said in March 7, 2006, Order Granting Mr. Leonetti's Petition Case No. 46369. The Proceedings at issue in this writ are 'Tortured.'

Compelling, convincing yet fearsome, and fraught with challenges. Stepping back from the harshness of Michael's language, he was an entertainer, a great chef and a decent human being. He never was, nor pretended to be, an attorney. The extent of his legal training commenced in prison with the jailhouse lawyers. It was the inmates who guided his legal defense, it was all he had and all he could afford. No outside attorney picked up the ball and tried to help an innocent man. No one listened to his cries for help, no one came to his rescue to undo such a heinous wrong. The only one on Michael's side was God, but God couldn't draft pleadings.

Michael continued to file a plethora of motions. His goal was to show the Court that it was his attorney who broke the law and in doing so, this should free Michael. But none of those highly charged emotional motions did the trick and released him from the horrors of prison life.

Michael drafted a pleading with the assistance of his fellow inmates. He believed this would persuade the Courts to review his case and set him free.

DECEIT CORRUPTION COVER-UP

DISTRICT OFFICES	STATE OF NEVADA	KENNY C. GUINN
1301 CORDONE AVE ☐ RENO, NEVADA 89502 (775) 688-1000		GOVERNOR RICHARD KIRKLAND DIRECTOR
A. A. CAMPOS BUILDING ☐ 215 E. BONANZA ROAD LAS VEGAS, NEVADA 89101 (702) 486-3001	**DEPARTMENT OF MOTOR VEHICLES AND PUBLIC SAFETY** DIVISION OF PAROLE AND PROBATION	
3920 E. IDAHO STREET ☐ ELKO, NEVADA 89801 (775) 738-4088		CLAY THOMAS, ACTING CHIEF 1445 HOT SPRINGS ROAD, NO. 104 ☒ CARSON CITY, NEVADA 89706 (775) 687-5040
119 E. LONG STREET ☐ CARSON CITY, NEVADA 89706 (775) 687-5045		

May 19, 2000

MICHAEL LEONETTI BIONDO
6287 FAIRBANKS
LAS VEGAS NV 89103

Dear Mr. Biondo:

After reviewing information contained within your file, it is found that your conviction does not meet the registration requirements set forth per the mandates of N.R.S. 179D. Therefore, this Division will be closing our record and destroying your file.

If you have any questions, you may contact the Sex Offender Registration Unit at (702) 684-2648 Monday through Friday, 8:00 a.m. to 5:00 p.m.

Sincerely,

Sex Offender Registration Unit
NV Division of Parole & Probation

cc: Misc. Correspondence
    DIV SOR Unit
    Las Vegas Metro Police Dept.
    James E. Guesman, Attorney

MICHAEL LEONETTI

Michael A. Root, ESQ., P.C.
Attorney At Law
612 S. TENTH ST. • LAS VEGAS, NV 89101 • (702) 382-2055 • FAX (702) 386-1979

July 25, 2000

LV Metro. Police
Risk Management Div.
714 S. Fourth St.
Las Vegas, NV 89101

Re: Your Ins.   : Las Vegas Metropolitan Police Dept.
        D/L   : 3/24/00
        Our client   : **MICHAEL LEONETTI**

Dear Sir:

    I represent MICHAEL and DIANE LEONETTI with regard to the below concern.

    The Leonettis advise that the facts are as follows.

    Michael and Diane Leonetti, husband and wife, are owners of LAS VEGAS IMAGE MAGAZINE, a local successful magazine, and they are law-abiding citizens of this state.

    The Leonettis are friends with the Conway family, and Mr. Leonetti sometimes drove CHELSEA CONWAY, a teenager, to school. Chelsea looks upon the Leonettis as family.

    Apparently, in early March, 2000, the police received an anonymous tip stating that Mr. Leonetti was having an "affair" with Chelsea. Immediately afterward, in early March, 2000, the police questioned Chelsea about this allegation, and were flatly informed in unmistakable terms that there was absolutely no truth to it. The Leonettis later discovered that the likely source of this outrageous slander was an emotionally disturbed teenage girl who was jealous of Chelsea.

    On March 24, 2000, DETECTIVE JENSEN appeared in Mr. Leonetti's business office and without an arrest warrant he arrested Mr. Leonetti in front of his wife, Diane, his daughter, Elaina, and their staff. Also in the office was a man who was negotiating to advertise in the Leonetti's magazine, and the Magazine's photographer and his wife. (See enclosures 1 and 2, Affidavits of CHASSIE HALSEY and ELSA RUSSO). Jensen's only stated ground for arrest was that Mr. Leonetti failed to register as a Felony sex offender. At the point of arrest, Mr. and Mrs. Leonetti attempted to convince Detective Jensen that he was never convicted

DECEIT CORRUPTION COVER-UP

LVMP Risk Management
July 26, 2000
page 2

of either a Felony or a sexual offense. Jensen stated to the Leonettis that he had been verbally told by the Lake Havasu, Arizona police that Mr. Leonetti was a felony sexual offender, and that Detective Jensen, who had no documents of any kind, stated: "I don't need any paperwork. I have my facts straight."

Mr. Leonetti spent twenty eight (28) hours in Jail, lost three hundred dollars ($300.00) for payment for a bail bond, and this incident was devastating to him and his family. In addition, Mr. Leonetti lost the advertising account as mentioned supra. Finally, the unjustified specter of being accused of a sexual molestation offense still haunts him and his family.

Further, when Diane Leonetti drove to retrieve her husband from jail to take him home, she was so distraught that she was involved in an automobile accident in which her neck was injured. She advises that she was in such a hurry to see and retrieve her husband from jail that an accident occurred. Obviously, there would have been no accident but for the fact of the unjust arrest.

Enclosures 3 and 4 verify that in 1993 Mr. Leonetti was convicted in Arizona of a misdemeanor, aggravated assault/unspecified offense. Please note that this conviction was not for a Felony, and was not a sexual offense. Please note that this information was obtained from the Las Vegas Metropolitan Records Section on March 27, 2000, and was therefore freely available to Detective Jensen at the point of arrest.

In addition, enclosure 5 conclusively proves that according to the Nevada Division of Parole and Probation, and in accordance with the Leonetti's claim to Detective Jensen at the point of arrest, Mr. Leonetti had no legal obligation of any kind to register with the State of Nevada.

Therefore, the facts evidence that Mr. Leonetti, without any cause, was unjustly and falsely arrested by Detective Jensen, an employee of the Las Vegas Metropolitan Police, which is a political subdivision of the State of Nevada. Because Detective Jensen failed to investigate or heed the nature of Mr. Leonetti's prior minor conviction, or obtain copies thereof, he was at least grossly negligent and at worst malicious when he arrested Mr. Leonetti. It is interesting to note that even a cursory look at Mr. Leonetti's LVMP record sheet evidences that Mr. Leonetti was not required to register in Nevada:

LVMP Risk Management
July 26, 2000
page 3

93 AZ 121994 **NOT REQ T/REG*MISD**

Even a cursory glance at Mr. Leonetti's record sheet would have revealed that no probable cause existed to arrest him. We have also been advised that standard police procedure prior to an arrest of this type is to obtain hard copies of any prior conviction of the suspect. The failure to do so was an unexplained deviation from standard police procedure.

Because there was no probable cause nor arrest warrant for Mr. Leonetti's arrest, this was a violation of 42 USC 1983, as it was a 4th and 14th Constitutional Rights violation of Mr. Leonetti's right to be free from unreasonable search and seizure. In addition, Detective Jensen's failure to investigate, to obtain an arrest warrant, indifference to the Leonetti's claims, and his statements to the Leonetti's and others during and after the arrest, support an intentional disregard or intentional dislike for Mr. Leonetti, and an intention to jail him for no cause. These facts more than fulfil the intent requirement of a 42 USC 1983 violation. To state the matter bluntly, The Leonettis believe, and the facts evidence that Detective Jensen, with full knowledge of the minor nature of Mr. Leonetti's prior misdemeanor conviction, intentionally jailed Mr. Leonetti because he did not like him. To jail a man for no reason is the quintessential violation of 42 USC 1983.

Accordingly, Mr. Leonetti presents his claim for $250,000 for your review.

Please contact me with regard to your position in this matter.

Sincerely,

MICHAEL A. ROOT, ESQ.

JAMES GUESMAN, ESQ.

MAR/ln
cc: client
encl: as stated.

DECEIT CORRUPTION COVER-UP

Law offices of
Michael A. Root, P. C.
A Professional Corporation
551 Gass Avenue • Las Vegas, Nevada 89101 • (702) 382-2055 • Fax (702) 386-1979

August 3, 2005

MICHAEL LEONETTI
NDOC #67009
Southern Desert Correctional Center
P.O. Box 208
Indian Springs, NV 89070

Via U.S. Mail

Dear Mr. Leonetti:

In response to your July 28, 2005 letter to me is the following.

The July 25, 2000 letter you have is the same as mine. I checked my file, and I do not have a signed copy. However, by this notarized letter, and as I am the custodian of my own records:

    1. That at all time herein affiant was and is a citizen of the United States, over 18 years of age, and competent to testify as averred below.

    2. That I am the President and Secretary of MICHAEL A. ROOT, PROF. CORP., and in such capacity I am the custodian of the records of that Corporation, and I am the management officer responsible for the collection, maintenance, and filing of all business paperwork generated and received by said corporation in the ordinary and usual course of its business.

    3. The three page attached letter dated July 25, 2000 is a true and accurate copy of the original that I sent to LVMPD on July 25, 2000.

SUBSCRIBED and SWORN to before
me this 3 day of August 20 05

NOTARY PUBLIC in and for
said COUNTY OF CLARK,
STATE OF NEVADA

Sincerely,

MICHAEL A. ROOT, P.C.

MAR/lm
encl: 7.25.00 letter

Notary Public - State of Nevada
County of Clark
LISA S. MYERS-GAMBINI
My Appointment Expires
April 2, 2008

MICHAEL LEONETTI

DECD
JAMES E. GUESMAN, ESQ.
Nevada State Bar No. 1610
4225 Fidus Drive, Suite 206
Las Vegas, Nevada 89103
(702) 734-2573
Attorney for Plaintiff

Nov 16 9 14 AM '00

CLERK

DISTRICT COURT, FAMILY DIVISION
CLARK COUNTY, NEVADA

DIANE LEONETTI,

    Plaintiff,

vs.

MICHAEL LEONETTI,

    Defendant.
_____//

CASE NO: 026102
DEPT: D

Hearing Date: N/A
Hearing Time: N/A

DECREE OF DIVORCE

This cause having come regularly for ~~Summary Disposition of Divorce without~~ hearing before the above-entitled Court, and the Court having read the Affidavit of Resident Witness and the Affidavit of the Plaintiff on file herein, and the cause having been submitted for decision for and judgment, and the Court being fully advised as to the law and the facts of the case, **FINDS**:

That the Court has complete jurisdiction in the premises both as to the subject matter thereof and the parties thereto; that the Plaintiff is now and has been an actual, bona fide, resident of the County of Clark, State of Nevada, and has been actually domiciled therein for more than six weeks immediately preceding the commencement of this action; that each and every one of the allegations contained in the Plaintiff's Complaint is true as therein alleged; that there is one minor child born of this marriage and that the Plaintiff, to her knowledge, is not pregnant; that the Plaintiff and has attended the COPE program; that the parties waive any rights to spousal support; that the parties have become so widely divergent and separated that the parties have become incompatible; that there is no possibility of reconciliation between them; that the parties waive their respective rights to written notice of entry of the Decree of Divorce, to appeal, to request Findings of Facts and Conclusions of Law and to move for a trial, and that the parties desire that the Court enter a Decree of Divorce.

NOW THEREFORE, IT IS HEREBY ORDERED, ADJUDGED AND DECREED that the bonds of matrimony now and heretofore existing between the Plaintiff and the Defendant are dissolved, set aside and forever held for naught, and that the parties are granted an absolute and final Decree of Divorce, and that each of the parties hereto is restored to the status of single, unmarried person.

IT IS FURTHER ORDERED, ADJUDGED AND DECREED that there is one (1) minor child born the issue of this marriage, to wit: ELAINE DEE LEONETTI, born April 18, 1989. There are no other minor children adopted during the marriage and Plaintiff is not currently pregnant.

IT IS FURTHER ORDERED, ADJUDGED AND DECREED that the Plaintiff shall have sole legal custody and primary physical custody of said minor child, to wit: ELAINE DEE LEONETTI, born April 18, 1989.

IT IS FURTHER ORDERED, ADJUDGED AND DECREED that due to the Defendant being incarcerated for crimes related to a minor-aged child, he shall not be entitled to have visitation with the parties' child during his incarceration.

IT IS FURTHER ORDERED, ADJUDGED AND DECREED that should Defendant be paroled while the child is still minor aged, then his visitation with the child shall be permitted only with supervision and solely at the discretion of Plaintiff.

IT IS FURTHER ORDERED, ADJUDGED AND DECREED that this case be sealed by the Court.

IT IS FURTHER ORDERED, ADJUDGED AND DECREED that Plaintiff has attended the COPE class and filed proof of her completion with the Court. The Defendant has not completed the COPE class, therefore, any visitation with the minor child he may be entitled to shall be suspended, until such times as he files proof of his COPE completion with the Court.

IT IS FURTHER ORDERED, ADJUDGED AND DECREED that the Defendant shall pay monthly child support to the Plaintiff in the amount of One Hundred Dollars ($100.00) per month, or eighteen percent (18%) of his gross monthly income, whichever is greater, but not less than the statutory minimum of $100.00 per month per child, until such time as the minor child attains the age of 18 years of age, if no longer enrolled in high school, otherwise, when the child reaches 19 years of age, pursuant to Nevada Revised Statute 125.510, marries, dies, or becomes otherwise emancipated. Said sum is consistent with N.R.S. 125.510.

IT IS FURTHER ORDERED, ADJUDGED AND DECREED that, pursuant to N.R.S. Chapter 125, notice is hereby given to the custodial parent or the parents having joint legal custody, that if you intend to move to a place outside the State and to take the minor children with you, must, as soon as possible and before the planned move, obtain the written consent of the other parent and if permission is refused, must obtain an Order from the Court to that effect.

PENALTY FOR VIOLATION OF ORDER: THE ABDUCTION, CONCEALMENT OR DETENTION OF A CHILD IN VIOLATION OF THIS ORDER IS PUNISHABLE AS A CATEGORY D FELONY AS PROVIDED IN NRS 193.130. NRS 200.359 provides that every person having a limited right of custody to a child or any parent having no right of custody to a child who willfully detains, conceals or removes the child from a parent, guardian or other person having lawful custody or a right of visitation of the child in violation of an order of this court, or removes the child from the jurisdiction of the court without the consent of either the court or all persons who have the right to custody or visitation is subject to being punished for a category D felony as provided in NRS 193.130.

IT IS FURTHER ORDERED, ADJUDGED AND DECREED that, pursuant to N.R.S. 125.450, notice is hereby given to the parent responsible for paying support that such person is subject to 31A of N.R.S. regarding the withholding of wages and commissions for payments of support. These statutes and provisions require that if an order issued by a Court of this or any other state, or pursuant to an expedited process, provides for payment for the support of a child, that order is a judgment by operation of law. Such a judgment may not be retroactively modified or adjusted and may be enforced as other judgments of this State. Thus, a parent responsible for paying child support shall be subject to having his or her wages or commission immediately subject to a Wage Assignment pursuant to the provisions of the above-cited statute upon presentation of said child support Order to said parent's employer.

IT IS FURTHER ORDERED, ADJUDGED AND DECREED that notice is hereby given, pursuant to N.R.S. 125B.145, that the Court is required to review child support obligations upon request by the parent, legal guardian or an attorney every three years to determine if the support being paid is within the formula of N.R.S. 125B.070.

IT IS FURTHER ORDERED, ADJUDGED AND DECREED that until otherwise ordered or agreed by the parties, the Plaintiff shall maintain medical insurance for said minor child, as long as it is available through her employment, and that the parties shall equally divide the costs of all medical, surgical, dental, orthodontic and optical expense of said minor child, including the cost of insurance and any deductibles, as well as any miscellaneous health related expenses incurred on behalf of said minor child not covered by insurance, until such time as said minor child attains the age of 18 years of age if no longer enrolled in high school, otherwise, when the child reaches 19 years of age, pursuant to Nevada Revised Statute 125.510, marries, dies, or becomes otherwise emancipated.

IT IS FURTHER ORDERED, ADJUDGED AND DECREED that both parties are subject to the terms imposed by the HAGUE CONVENTION of October 25, 1985, adopted by the 14th Session of the Hague Conference on Private International Law, in accord with NRS 125.510 (7), and that the United States is the country and Nevada is the state of habitual residence of the minor child, in accordance with NRS 125.510(8) and NRS 125C.010.

IT IS FURTHER ORDERED, ADJUDGED AND DECREED that Plaintiff shall be entitled to claim any dependency exemption or deduction for income tax purposes attributable to the support of the minor child, under Section 151 of the Internal Revenue Code, as amended, or the corresponding provisions of any successor statute.

IT IS FURTHER ORDERED, ADJUDGED AND DECREED that there is community property to be divided between the parties or adjudicated by the Court as follows:

To Plaintiff, free from any future claim by Defendant:

a. 1991 Cadillac Fleetwood, VIN # 1G6CB53B6M4279733, subject to encumbrance thereon;

b. 1985 Honda Shadow motorcycle, VIN # JH2RC190SFM13019;

c. The marital residence, located at 6287 Fairbanks Drive, Las Vegas, Nevada 89103, subject to the encumbrance thereon;

d. Musical instruments, recreational equipment, tools and equipment, currently in her possession;

e. Any interest past or present in the business known as Las Vegas Image Magazine, Inc., subject to the encumbrance thereon;

    f. Any and all banking accounts currently in her name;

    g. All furniture and furnishings currently in her possession; and

    h. All of her jewelry, personal possessions and belongings.

IT IS FURTHER ORDERED, ADJUDGED AND DECREED that there are community debts and obligations to be allocated as follows:

To be assumed by Plaintiff, holding Defendant harmless therefrom:

    a. Encumbrance on the marital residence located at 6287 Fairbanks Drive, Las Vegas, Nevada 89103;

    b. Business debts associated with Las Vegas Image Magazine; and

    c. Encumbrance on the 1991 Cadillac Fleetwood.

IT IS FURTHER ORDERED, ADJUDGED AND DECREED that no spousal support is to be paid to or by either of the parties now or in the future. Both parties understand that this waiver is permanent and that they may not petition the court for such relief.

IT IS FURTHER ORDERED, ADJUDGED AND DECREED that, except as provided for herein, the parties waive any and all right each may have as to the other party's retirement, pension, 401K and/or IRA, if any.

IT IS FURTHER ORDERED, ADJUDGED AND DECREED that the Plaintiff desires to maintain her married name, to wit: DIANE LEONETTI.

IT IS FURTHER ORDERED, ADJUDGED AND DECREED that the parties shall execute any and all documents necessary to achieve the provisions of this Decree.

DATED this _____ day of __NOV 1 6 2000__ 2000.

                                            DISTRICT JUDGE

Respectfully submitted by: Approved as to form and content:

JAMES E. GUESMAN, ESQ.   MICHAEL LEONETTI, Defendant
Nevada State Bar No. 1610   In Proper Person
Attorney for Plaintiff

VERIFICATION

STATE OF NEVADA)
) ss:
COUNTY OF CLARK)

MICHAEL LEONETTI, being first duly sworn, deposes and says:

That he is the Defendant in the above-entitled matter, that he has read the foregoing Decree of Divorce and knows the contents thereof; that the same is true of his own knowledge, except for those matters therein stated on information and belief, and as to those matters, he believes them to be true.

MICHAEL LEONETTI

SUBSCRIBED AND SWORN to before me this _16th_ day of October, 2000.

NOTARY PUBLIC in and for said County and State

*Notary Public - State of Nevada
County of Clark
MARTY KING
My Appointment Expires
September 29, 2003
No: 99-42768-1*

ACKNOWLEDGMENT

STATE OF NEVADA)
) ss:
COUNTY OF CLARK)

On this _16th_ day of _October_, 2000, personally appeared before me, a Notary Public in and for said County and State, MICHAEL LEONETTI, known to me to be the person described herein and who executed the foregoing Answer in Proper Person, who acknowledged to me that the same was executed freely and voluntarily and for the uses and purposes therein mentioned.

NOTARY PUBLIC in and for said County and State

*Notary Public - State of Nevada
County of Clark
MARTY KING
My Appointment Expires
September 29, 2003
No: 99-42768-1*

- 6 -

Case Nos. 99-100-0291, 00-049-0291, 90-055-0291, 00-056-0291, 00-057-0039, 01-045-0291

STATE BAR OF NEVADA
SOUTHERN NEVADA DISCIPLINARY BOARD

FILED
MAY 15 2001
T. Slaughter
STATE BAR OF NEVADA

STATE BAR OF NEVADA
Complainant,

vs.

JAMES E. GUESMAN, ESQ.
Respondent.

CONDITIONAL GUILTY PLEA IN EXCHANGE FOR A STATED FORM OF DISCIPLINE

The undersigned, JAMES E. GUESMAN, ESQ., a duly licensed attorney with the State Bar of Nevada (hereafter "State Bar"), and named Respondent herein, by and through his counsel J.D. Evans, Esq., hereby tenders to Bar Counsel pursuant to SCR 113(1) the following Conditional Guilty Plea Agreement in Exchange for a Stated Form of Discipline:

I.

CONDITIONAL GUILTY PLEA

Respondent pleads guilty to violating SCR 79 (Address of member), SCR 151 (Competence), SCR 153 (Diligence), 154 (Communication), SCR 173(3) (Fairness to opposing party and counsel), SCR 187 (Responsibility regarding nonlawyer assistants) and Knowingly disobeying an obligation under the rules of a tribunal. SCR 200(2)(Bar association and disciplinary matters: failure to respond to a lawful request for information from a disciplinary authority) as set forth below in the Stipulation of Facts:

II.

STIPULATION OF FACTS

A. September 26, 2000 Formal Complaint

COUNT 1
State Bar file no. 99-100-0291/Povelko, Leslie

1. In March of 1998, Leslie Povelko (hereafter "Povelko") retained Respondent for $750.00 to assist her with child support and visitation matters concerning her daughter.

2. Shortly after retaining Respondent, Povelko began experiencing problems with their professional relationship and with Respondent's secretary. Specifically, Povelko was not notified of case status.

3. Consequently, Povelko reported Respondent to the State Bar. In attempting to investigate Povelko's allegations, the State Bar sent numerous letters to Respondent eliciting information. Though Respondent requested and was granted extensions of time to provide a response, Respondent failed to respond.

4. In light of the foregoing, Respondent violated SCR 154 (Communication) and SCR 200(2) (Bar association and disciplinary matters: failure to respond to a lawful request for information from a disciplinary authority). Respondent also admits to violating SCR 187 (Responsibility regarding nonlawyer assistants), though not specifically charged in the State Bar's Complaint.

COUNT 2

State Bar File No. 00-049-0291/Sheldon, BettyJane

1. In August of 1996, BettyJane Sheldon (hereafter "Sheldon") retained Respondent to represent her in her divorce. Upon retention, Sheldon remitted payment to Respondent's paralegal, "Paula."

2. For the next five months, Sheldon did not receive return telephone calls from Respondent's office and never received a copy of her divorce decree.

3. Sometime thereafter, Sheldon was advised that Respondent no longer employed Paula. Sheldon was further advised that the firm hired a new paralegal named "Tamberlie," who would be assisting Respondent and would follow up with Sheldon.

4. Sheldon remained patient for the next several months, but heard nothing from Respondent's office. Thereafter, she resumed calling Respondent's office and eventually reached Respondent in May of 1999.

MICHAEL LEONETTI

5. Thereafter, Respondent failed to maintain adequate communication with Sheldon. In attempting to determine the status of her case, Sheldon contacted the Family Court Clerk's Office and was advised that a complaint for divorce was never filed.

6. Consequently, Sheldon reported Respondent to the State Bar. In attempting to investigate Sheldon's allegations, the State Bar sent numerous letters to Respondent. Respondent failed to respond.

7. In light of the foregoing, Respondent violated SCR 154 (Communication) and SCR 200(2) (Bar association and disciplinary matters: failure to respond to a lawful request for information from a disciplinary authority). Respondent also admits to violating SCR 187 (Responsibility regarding nonlawyer assistants), though not specifically charged in the State Bar's Complaint.

COUNT 3

State Bar File No. 00-055-0291/Stockett, Larry

This Count is dismissed in its entirety by agreement between the parties herein.

COUNT 4

State Bar File No. 00-056-0291/Haney, Kathleen

1. Kathleen Haney (hereafter "Haney") retained Respondent in 1994 to represent her in an auto accident case.

2. In July of 1997, Haney filed a grievance against Respondent with the State Bar complaining that Respondent performed little or no legal services on her behalf and failed to maintain adequate communication with her.

3. In a September 4, 1997, letter, Respondent stated to Bar Counsel that he timely filed a civil complaint on Haney's behalf to "preserve the Statute Deadline."

4. Based on Respondent's representations in his September 1997 letter, Patrice Eichman (then Assistant Bar Counsel) closed the matter.

5. On January 28, 2000, Respondent notified the State Bar via telephone that his

STATE BAR OF NEVADA
SOUTHERN NEVADA DISCIPLINARY BOARD

IN RE: DISCIPLINE OF
JAMES E. GUESMAN, ESQ.

_____/

PUBLIC REPRIMAND

On May 15, 2001, a Hearing Panel of the Southern Nevada Disciplinary Board convened to review the above-captioned matters. At that proceeding, Respondent tendered a Conditional Guilty Plea in Exchange for a Stated Form of Discipline wherein he accepted, among other conditions, the issuance of a Public Reprimand. See SCR 113.

The Hearing Panel having approved Respondent's Conditional Plea, the following Public Reprimand is hereby issued in accordance with SCR 113(5):

To: **JAMES E. GUESMAN, ESQ.**

This Public Reprimand is the culmination of five (5) grievances lodged against you for professional misconduct. Much of the professional misconduct may be attributable to a lack of adequate supervision on your part of your nonlawyer staff. A summary of those grievances is as follows:

(1) In August of 1996, you were retained by BettyJane Sheldon (hereafter "Sheldon") to represent her in her divorce. Upon retention, Sheldon remitted payment to your paralegal. For the next five months, Sheldon did not receive return telephone calls from your office and did not receive a copy of her divorce decree.

Sometime thereafter, Sheldon was advised that you no longer employed your paralegal. Sheldon was further advised that the firm hired a new paralegal who would be assisting you and would follow up with Sheldon.

Sheldon remained patient for the several months thereafter, but heard nothing from your office. She resumed calling your office and eventually reached you in May of 1999.

Thereafter, you failed to maintain adequate communication with Sheldon. In attempting to determine the status of her case, Sheldon contacted the Family Court Clerk's Office and was advised that a complaint for divorce was never filed.

III.

STATED FORM OF DISCIPLINE

As a result of his conditional guilty plea contained herein, Respondent agrees to the imposition of professional discipline as set forth below:

1. Pursuant to SCR 113(5), Respondent shall receive a public reprimand for the foregoing Rule violations, a draft of which is attached hereto. **Exhibit 1.**

2. Respondent shall be placed on probation for two (2) years, the terms of which are as follows:

   a. Respondent shall complete six (6) extra continuing legal education ("CLE") credits over and above that which he is already required to complete pursuant to SCR 210. Any of the following categories of CLE shall satisfy this condition: Ethics, civil procedure, appellate procedure, criminal procedure and/or law office management.

   b. Respondent shall provide to the State Bar quarterly reports from a licensed psychologist or psychiatrist attesting to the fact that Respondent has been evaluated at least one (1) time during that quarter and that he is mentally and emotionally competent to practice law.

   c. Within thirty (30) days of receiving the State Bar's bill of costs for the investigation and prosecution of this matter, Respondent shall make payment in full for all costs contained therein. Costs include any and all court reporting services, as well as any postal or service of process costs incurred.

3. In the event Respondent violates any of the foregoing probationary conditions or is the subject of any professional discipline arising out of misconduct perpetrated during his probationary period, the designated hearing panel shall retain jurisdiction and may reconvene for further disciplinary proceedings, including the possible imposition of a suspension, upon motion by bar counsel.

. . .
. . .
. . .

IV.

STATE BAR'S AGREEMENT

1. The State Bar agrees to dismiss and recommends dismissal of the following:

    a. SCR 153 of Count 1 of the September 26, 2000 formal Complaint;

    b. SCR 151, SCR 153 and SCR 200(2) of Count 2 of the September 26, 2000 formal Complaint;

    c. Count 3 in its entirety, of the September 26, 2000 formal Complaint;

    d. SCR 166(4), SCR 200(1) and SCR 203(3) of Count 4 of the September 26, 2000 formal Complaint;

    e. SCR 165, SCR 166(4) and SCR 200(2) of Count 5 of the September 26, 2000 formal Complaint; and,

    f. SCR 151, 153 and 203(4) of the April 24, 2001 formal Complaint.

2. The State Bar waives reimbursement of any State Bar staff salaries expended toward the investigation or prosecution of this matter.

3. The State Bar recommends that the Panel consider, as a mitigating circumstance, the fact that Respondent suffered from depression during the relevant times herein.

4. The State Bar agrees to the Stated Form of Discipline set forth above.

V.

APPROVAL BY RESPONDENT AND HIS COUNSEL

Having read the Conditional Guilty Plea in Exchange for a Stated Form of Discipline and being satisfied with it, the undersigned hereby approve and recommend approval of the same by the Southern Nevada Disciplinary Board.

Dated this 15th of May, 2001.

JAMES E. GUESSMAN, ESQ.
Nevada Bar No. 001610
P.O. Box 230100
Las Vegas, Nevada 89123
RESPONDENT

Dated this 15th of May, 2001.

J.D. EVANS, ESQ.
Nevada Bar No. 002267
3607 W. Charleston Blvd.
Las Vegas, Nevada 89102
(702) 880-1211

ATTORNEY FOR RESPONDENT

VI.

APPROVAL BY BAR COUNSEL

Having read the Conditional Guilty Plea in Exchange for a Stated Form of Discipline and being satisfied with it, the undersigned hereby approves and recommends approval of the same by the Southern Nevada Disciplinary Board.

Dated this 15th of May, 2001.

STATE BAR OF NEVADA
ROB W. BARE, BAR COUNSEL

MICHAEL J. WARHOLA, Assistant Bar Counsel
Nevada Bar No. 005814
600 E. Charleston Blvd.
Las Vegas, Nevada 89104
(702) 382-2200

ATTORNEY FOR COMPLAINANT

5. Thereafter, Respondent failed to maintain adequate communication with Sheldon. In attempting to determine the status of her case, Sheldon contacted the Family Court Clerk's Office and was advised that a complaint for divorce was never filed.

6. Consequently, Sheldon reported Respondent to the State Bar. In attempting to investigate Sheldon's allegations, the State Bar sent numerous letters to Respondent. Respondent failed to respond.

7. In light of the foregoing, Respondent violated SCR 154 (Communication) and SCR 200(2) (Bar association and disciplinary matters: failure to respond to a lawful request for information from a disciplinary authority). Respondent also admits to violating SCR 187 (Responsibility regarding nonlawyer assistants), though not specifically charged in the State Bar's Complaint.

COUNT 3

State Bar File No. 00-055-0291/Stockett, Larry

This Count is dismissed in its entirety by agreement between the parties herein.

COUNT 4

State Bar File No. 00-056-0291/Haney, Kathleen

1. Kathleen Haney (hereafter "Haney") retained Respondent in 1994 to represent her in an auto accident case.

2. In July of 1997, Haney filed a grievance against Respondent with the State Bar complaining that Respondent performed little or no legal services on her behalf and failed to maintain adequate communication with her.

3. In a September 4, 1997, letter, Respondent stated to Bar Counsel that he timely filed a civil complaint on Haney's behalf to "preserve the Statute Deadline."

4. Based on Respondent's representations in his September 1997 letter, Patrice Eichman (then Assistant Bar Counsel) closed the matter.

5. On January 28, 2000, Respondent notified the State Bar via telephone that his

DECEIT CORRUPTION COVER-UP

Consequently, Sheldon reported you to the State Bar. In attempting to investigate Sheldon's allegations, the State Bar sent numerous letters to you. However, you failed to respond.

In light of the foregoing, the designated panel found violated SCR 154 (Communication), SCR 187 (Responsibility regarding nonlawyer assistants) and SCR 200(2) (Bar association and disciplinary matters: failure to respond to a lawful request for information from a disciplinary authority).

(2) In March of 1998, Leslie Povelko (hereafter "Povelko") retained you assist her with child support and visitation matters concerning her daughter. Shortly after you were retained, Povelko began experiencing problems with your office.

Specifically, Povelko was not notified of the case status by your secretary. Consequently, Povelko reported you to the State Bar. In attempting to investigate Povelko's allegations, the State Bar sent numerous letters to you eliciting information. Though you requested and were granted extensions of time to provide a response, you failed to respond.

In light of the foregoing, the designated panel found that you violated SCR 154 (Communication), SCR 187 (Responsibility regarding nonlawyer assistants) and SCR 200(2) (Bar association and disciplinary matters: failure to respond to a lawful request for information from a disciplinary authority).

(3) In 1994, Kathleen Haney (hereafter "Haney") retained you to represent her in an auto accident case. In July of 1997, Haney filed a grievance against you with the State Bar complaining that you performed little or no legal services on her behalf and failed to maintain adequate communication with her.

In a September 4, 1997, letter, you advised the State Bar that you timely filed a civil complaint on Haney's behalf to "preserve the Statute Deadline." Based on your representations in your September 1997 letter, the matter was closed.

In January 1998, you notified the State Bar via telephone that your prior letter was inaccurate because, though you timely filed suit, you did not effectuate service upon the defendant within the 120 day time frame set forth in the NRCP. Consequently, the suit was time barred because you could no longer re-file it during the applicable limitations period.

In light of the foregoing, the designated hearing panel found that you violated SCR 151 (Competence), SCR 153 (Diligence), SCR 154 (Communication) and SCR 187 (Responsibility regarding nonlawyer assistants).

(4) Patrick Baumgartner (hereafter "Baumgartner") retained you to represent him in his divorce. At the time, Baumgartner was stationed in Egypt but was home on emergency leave. He also retained you to draft and file the necessary documentation to secure an extension in Baumgartner's emergency leave so that he would be present for his divorce proceedings.

You drafted a complaint for divorce and had it verified by Baumgartner on or about June 24, 1998. You failed to file and serve Baumgartner's complaint for divorce. Consequently, Baumgartner had to retain new counsel as of August 14, 1998.

Your failure to file Baumgartner's complaint for divorce is, at least in part, due to your failure to adequately supervise your nonlawyer staff. Ultimately, you refunded Baumgartner's retainer in full.

In light of the foregoing, the designated hearing panel found that you violated SCR 151 (Competence), 153 (Diligence), SCR 154 (Communication) and SCR 187 (Responsibility regarding nonlawyer assistants).

(5) You were counsel of record for Michael Leonetti in his guilty plea resulting in a criminal conviction (*Leonetti v. State*, no. 36980).

During the course of an appeal, which was unknown to you at the time, you failed to respond to any of the notices and orders sent to you by the Supreme Court of Nevada. All written communication to you was returned to the Court. On March 26, 2001, the Supreme Court entered an order, which was served on you, remanding the case to District Court to secure new appellate counsel.

In light of the foregoing, the designated hearing panel found that you violated SCR 79 (Address of member) and SCR 173(3) (Knowingly disobeying an obligation under the rules of a tribunal).

Pursuant to the terms of your conditional guilty plea agreement, you are also hereby placed on probation for a period of two (2) years, with conditions as set forth in the Conditional Guilty Plea.

It is so ORDERED.

ELEISSA C. LAVELLE, ESQ., Panel Chair
Southern Nevada Disciplinary Board

DECEIT CORRUPTION COVER-UP

Case Nos. 99-100-0291, 00-049-0291, 00-55-0291, 00-56-291, 00-057-0039, 01-045-0291

STATE BAR OF NEVADA

SOUTHERN NEVADA DISCIPLINARY BOARD

FILED
MAY 30 2001
T. Slaughter
STATE BAR OF NEVADA

IN RE DISCIPLINE OF
JAMES E. GUESMAN, ESQ.
_____/

ORDER APPROVING CONDITIONAL GUILTY PLEA AND ADMINISTRATION OF PUBLIC REPRIMAND

This matter came before a designated Formal Hearing Panel of the Southern Nevada Disciplinary Board ("Panel") on May 15, 2001 for consideration of the Conditional Guilty Plea in Exchange for a Stated Form of Discipline ("Conditional Guilty Plea") of JAMES E. GUESMAN, ESQ., ("Respondent"), pursuant to Supreme Court Rule 113. The Panel consisted of Eleissa C. Lavelle, Esq., Chair, Kristina Sue Holman, Esq., Martin J. Kravitz, Esq., Paul E. Larsen, Esq., and Susan Krenzien, laymember.

The State Bar of Nevada was represented by Assistant Bar Counsel, Michael J. Warhola. Respondent was present and was represented by J. D. Evans, Esq..

Respondent tendered a Conditional Guilty Plea in Exchange for a Stated Form of Discipline ("Conditional Guilty Plea") pursuant to SCR 113 which was signed by Respondent and his counsel and was recommended for approval by Assistant Bar Counsel. Based upon the pleadings on file herein and the proposed Conditional Guilty Plea, the Panel issues the following Findings of Fact and Conclusions of Law:

FINDINGS OF FACT

1. Respondent is an attorney licensed to practice law in the State of Nevada whose principal office for practice of law is located in Clark County, Nevada. Respondent was admitted to practice law in the State of Nevada in December 1977;

2. On September 26, 2000, the State Bar of Nevada filed a five (5) count formal Complaint against Respondent charging him with violating SCR 151 (Competence), SCR 153 (Diligence), SCR 154 (Communication), SCR 165 (Safekeeping property), SCR 166(4) (Declining or terminating representation), SCR 187 (Responsibility regarding nonlawyer assistants), SCR 200(1) (Misrepresentations to a disciplinary authority), SCR 200(2) (Bar association and disciplinary matters) and SCR 203(3) (Misconduct: engaging in dishonesty, fraud, deceit or misrepresentation).

3. On April 24, 2001, the State Bar of Nevada filed a second formal Complaint against Respondent charging him with violating SCR 173(3) (Fairness to opposing party and counsel: knowingly disobeying an obligation under the rules of a tribunal) and SCR 203(4) (Misconduct: conduct prejudicial to the administration of justice).

4. On May 15, 2001, Respondent and the State Bar entered into a Conditional Guilty Plea pursuant to SCR 113, the terms of which are incorporated herein by reference.

5. The Stipulation of Facts as revised in the original Conditional Guilty Plea on file herein is incorporated in its entirety by reference herein and shall serve as the Findings of Fact to this Order.

CONCLUSIONS OF LAW

Based upon the foregoing Findings of Fact, the Panel hereby issues the following Conclusions of Law:

1. That the Southern Nevada Disciplinary Board has jurisdiction over Respondent and the subject matter of these proceedings pursuant to Supreme Court Rule 99;

DECEIT CORRUPTION COVER-UP

```
ORDR
MICHAEL H. SCHWARZ, ESQ.
Nevada Bar No. 5126
601 E. Charleston Blvd.
Las Vegas, Nevada 89104
(702) 598-3909
```

COPY

FILED

DISTRICT COURT

CLARK COUNTY, NEVADA

DIANE LEONETTI,

        Plaintiff,

vs.

MICHAEL LEONETTI,

        Defendant.

CASE NO: D261022-D

DEPT. NO: F

ORDER GRANTING DEFENDANT'S MOTION TO VACATE JUDGMENT

THIS MATTER having come on for hearing on the 6th day of February at the hour of 9:00 a.m., Attorney MICHAEL H. SCHWARZ, ESQ., appearing on behalf of the Defendant, MICHAEL LEONETTI and no appearance being made for the Plaintiff. The Court, after taking evidence, hearing testimony and **GOOD CAUSE APPEARING** it is,

HELD: That the Plaintiff received legal notice of the hearing on February 6, 2004, having been presented to Plaintiff's daughter at her residence and that the Plaintiff's lack of appearance was her choice; it is further

HELD: That the Court will not make a ruling as to the allegations of conflict between the Defendant and his Counsel, JAMES E. GUESMAN, ESQ., as this issue is currently before the Honorable Judge Jackie Glass; it is further

HELD: That evidence was presented at the Rule 60(b) Motion hearing which established that the Defendant requested psychiatric assistance and received it; that the Defendant was on psychiatric medications at the time that he signed the Divorce paperwork; that a past employee

EXHIBIT "5a" Case No. D261022

EX 5-A

of the Defendant testified that he believed that the thought processes of the Defendant had been affected while he was in custody, however, the witness was unable to establish at what point in the time line he believed this to be true; It is further

HELD: That there was no evidence presented that the Defendant was irrational at the time he was approached by his Attorney James Guesman to sign divorce paperwork; It is further

HELD: In this case, regarding the division of community property, the Plaintiff received everything. Not only was the distribution of community property disproportionate and unfair, it was unconscionable. The division of community property in this case flies in the face of current case law which favors an equal distribution of assets; it is further

HELD: That the disproportionate division cannot be justified or related to fault. Whether or not the Defendant committed a criminal act or not is irrelevant to the division of property. It is further

HELD: As to long period of time the Defendant waited before filing his **NRCP 60(b)** Motion, the Court finds that the totality of the circumstances involved in Defendant's signing, combined with the encumbrance of being incarcerated and the records indicating that psychiatric assistance was administered to the Defendant there appears to be justification for granting his Motion; Therefore it is

ORDERED: That the Decree of Divorce is set aside due to fraud in accordance with **NRCP 60(b)**; it is further

HELD: That the Court shall not set aside the divorce itself, however, the Court shall maintain jurisdiction on the issue of property distribution so that a fair and equitable distribution may be approached by the parties; It is further

HELD: That as to the Defendant's request to attend and complete COPE classes, it is

ORDERED: That the Defendant is to attend Parenting classes while in custody and completion of these classes shall be accepted by this Court in lieu of the COPE class requirement; It is further

. . .

. . .

. . .

DECEIT CORRUPTION COVER-UP

HELD: That it is either inappropriate or premature to address setting aside any other portions of the Decree at this time, as no evidence regarding other matters has been presented. However, when, and if, the Defendant is released from custody the Defendant may file the appropriate motion or motions at that time due to change in circumstances.

DATED and DONE this __11__ day of March, 2004.

SENIOR JUDGE JAMES A. BRENNAN
DISTRICT JUDGE

for- JUDGE ROBERT E. GASTON

Submitted by:
Attorney for the Defendant

MICHAEL H. SCHWARZ, ESQ.

CLERK

MAR 11 4 22 PM '04

MICHAEL LEONETTI

ROBERT KNIGHTON
750 EAST SIERRA VISTA DRIVE # 36
LAS VEGAS NEVADA, 89109

AFFIDAVIT OF ROBERT KNIGHTON

On April 2, 2004 I was to testify at the evidentiary hearing in court room 5 in front of Judge Jackie Glass, to my knowledge of the conspiracy that Diane Leonetti and James Guesman was plotting against Michael Leonetti, as I was sitting out in the hall of the court room that day with my daughter, Kristina Knighton we " heard " and seen James Guesman Esq. And Diane Leonetti talking that they wanted to have Michael Leonetti Killed or to have him killed in prison. My daughter and I were very worried and concerned, so my daughter and I went to the bailiff and told him what we heard. We also Told the bailiff that the Chaplin from the prison Ken Mellone also heard the conversation Between Diane Leonetti and Guesman, so he told the bailiff as well. When the bailiff Came back he told us that he told Judge Jackie Glass. We tried to explain to the bailiff That James Guesman and Diane Leonetti was conspiring to commit murder. The bailiff's Reply was " I told the Judge and **"that is that "**.it seemed that what was said was deliberately ignored. When it was my turn to testify Judge Jackie Glass was asking me all the questions, she ask me what I knew about the law and if I helped James Guesman. Put together the criminal case for Mr. Leonetti. I didn't know what that had to do with me Testifying of what I heard and seen in 2000 when Diane Leonetti and James Guesman Conspired to take all that Mr. Leonetti had. Also Diane Leonetti said that she would LIE! And do anything she can to put Michael Leonetti in prison, and to destroy him. Judge Glass did not let me speak she was very Bias and very rude and did not give me A chance to tell all that know of what I heard and seen to show that there was a conspiracy against Michael Leonetti from the beginning. Judge Glass was afraid that I would of put on the record what I heard in the hall way and seen, her job was to hear the truth but Judge Glass instead was to cover up and not to expose the ones that broken the law. I was I eye witness to what has been said about Michael Leonetti by Diane Leonetti and James Guesman also Betsy Allen, Mr. Leonetti Attorney spoke to very briefly that on

EXHIBIT "6"
EXHIBIT 6.

DECEIT CORRUPTION COVER-UP

April 2, 2004 she also did not care what I had to say. I felt it in my heart that something was wrong all that I have said in this affidavit is true. And I could testify that there is a conspiracy against Michael Leonetti., but I must be allowed to tell what I know of this horrible injustice that is taking place, and to put a innocent man in prison, when the ones that broke the law are FREE!.

Dated: This 30th day of August, 2004

Respectfully submitted

Robert Knighton

SUBSCRIBED and SWORN to, before me, _____

NOTARY PUBLIC
MY COMMISSION EXPIRES
April 9, 2007

A NOTARY PUBLIC, in the STATE of: Idaho, in and for the COUNTY OF BONNER

of: Bonner ; DATED: This 30th day of August, 2004

"6"

MICHAEL LEONETTI

KRISTINA KNIGHTON
750 EAST SIERRA VISTA DRIVE # 36
LAS VEGAS NEVADA, 89109

AFFIDAVIT OF KRISTINA KNIGHTON

On April 2, 2004 I went with my father to court to see Michael Leonetti, as I was sitting with my father out side of the court room. I also heard Diane Leonetti and James Guesman say that they wanted to have Michael Leonetti "KILLED", or have him killed in prison. I was very scared and afraid for him, so my father went to the bailiff and told him what we heard, even the Chaplin that was there for Michael Leonetti heard what was said. And he told the bailiff also, but when the bailiff came back he said that he told the judge. But the bailiff seemed that he did not care, and walked away from us.

Respectfully Submitted

Kristina Knighton

SUBSCRIBED and SWORN to, before me. _Lorraine Bennett_

NOTARY PUBLIC

A NOTARY PUBLIC, IN THE STATE OF: _Idaho_, in and for the

COUNTY of: _Bonner_ : Dated This _30th_ day of August, 2004

EXHIBIT "7"

DECEIT CORRUPTION COVER-UP

kristys affidavit for mike

Affidavidt of Kristina Marie Knighton

On or about April 02, 2004, I was in the courtroom hallwawy when I overheard a conversation with Diane Leonetti, attorney James Guesman and another man, Don Rux, (Diane's Father.)

I was sitting with my father Robert Knighton when we both overheard conversation between Diane, James and Don. They were very upset after Diane's testimony.

Diane had stated that she was sick and tired on all of the s**t that Michael was putting her through. Attorney Guesman had made a comment that he knew somebody in the prison that would be able to take care of this for him. Dianes's father, Don, said to get things started that he (Don) would get whatever money together to pay for the "hit".

This conversation had taken place during which time the court's bailiff was initially told of what my father Robert and I had heard which caused the bailiff to notify Judge Glass of what had been overheard.

Kristina Marie Knighton

I declare under penalty of purgury that the above affidavit is true and correct to the best f my knowledge.

Dated this 20th day of April, 2005 *Kristina M. Knighton*

Melissa KE
NOTARY PUBLIC

MELISSA KAYE EASON
NOTARY PUBLIC
STATE OF NEVADA
APPT. No. 04-89989-14
MY APPT. EXPIRES JUNE 11, 2008

EXHIBIT "7a"

MICHAEL LEONETTI

Michael Leonetti #67009
Southern Desert Correctional Center
Post Office Box 208
Indian Springs, Nevada
89070-0208
Attorney Pro Se

UNITED STATES DISTRICT COURT
SOUTHERN DISTRICT OF NEVADA

MICHAEL LEONETTI,

        Petitioner,

Vs:

The State of Nevada
Judge Jackie Glass

        Respondent,

Case No. 2:07-CV-0236-KJD-RJJ
District Court No. C-169467

MEMORANDUM

COMES NOW, PETITIONER MICHAEL LEONETTI, IN HIS PROPER PERSON MEMORANDUM TO JUDGE JACKIE GLASS EIGHTH DISTRICT COURT TO RESIGN FROM THE BENCH AND TO TURN HERSELF IN TO THE THE PROPER AUTHORITES.

DATED THIS 7th DAY OF SEPTEMBER 2007

        Respectfully submitted

        Michael Leonetti #67009
        Southern Desert Correctional Center
        Post Office Box 208
        Indian Springs, Nevada 89070-0208
        Attorney Pro Se

DECEIT CORRUPTION COVER-UP

Michael Leonetti 367009
Southern Desert Correctional Center
Post Office Box 208
Indian Springs, Nevada
89070-0208

September 7, 2007

To: Judge Jackie Glass
200 Lewis Ave. 3rd Floor
Las Vegas, Nevada
89155

CASE NO. 2:07-CV-0236-KJD-RJJ

DISTRICT COURT NO. C-169467

RE: RESIGNATION FROM THE BENCH AND TO TURN
YOURSELF IN TO THE PROPER AUTHORITES

Dear Judge Glass,

    You were assined this case on January 8, 2004 you went against the Orders of the Supreme Court's August 20, 2002 Order of Reversal and Remand CASE NO. 39531. You refused to here the May 9, 2001 Habeas Corpus Petition Appellant's May 9, 2001 Motion to withdraw the Guilty Plea, and ALL of the subsequent documents filed by the appellant in effort to litigate his petition and Motion.

    You have done all you can to sweep under the rug the criminal Conduct that was done to me by the State of Nevada in my case to protect and hide the false arrest that was done to me by the Las Vegas Police Dept. in MARCH of 2000.

    EXHIBIT A
Is a copy of the July 25, 2000 letter and claim for $250.000.00 thousand dollars that was sent to Las Vegas Metro Police Risk Div. 714 South Fourth Street Las Vegas, Nevada 89101.

    You have been aware of this document Judge John S. McGroarty the District Attorney Stewert Bell.... also knew about this. But all of you choose to hide this information.

    EXHIBIT B
May 19, 2000 letter from Division of Parloe and Probation.

On April 2, 2004 there was a evidentiry hearing, you heard that hearing in a NARROW SCOPE, that is not what the Supreme Court's ORDER said of August 20, 2002 the ORDER said; **ALL DOCUMENTS...** You stated on the April 2, 2004 hearing on the record page 51 line 12 and 13;

    " **I DON'T BELIEVE THERE WAS A CONFLICT. I ALSO BELIEVE THAT MR. GUESMAN ACTED APPROPRIATELY WHEN HE RECEIVED THE WAIVER THAT WAS SIGNED BY MR. LEONETTI.**

On August 7, 2007 the Supreme Court ORDER OF AFFIRMANCE CASE NO. 47485 stated;

1.

MICHAEL LEONETTI

" WE CONCLUDE THAT LEONETTI DEMONSTRATED THAT AN ACTUAL CONFLICT OF INTEREST EXISTED WITH REGARD TO GUESMAN'S REPRESENTATION OF DIANE LEONETTI: THE RECORED REVEALS THAT GUESMAN SIMULTANEOUSLY REPRESENTED MICHAEL LEONETTI IN THE CRIMINAL MATTER AND DIANE LEONETTI IN HER DIVORCE PROCEEDING AGAINST MICHAEL LEONETTI, ALTHOUGH GUESMAN HAD LEONETTI SIGN A WAIVER OF THE CONFLICT, THE WAIVER WAS NOT PRESENTED TO LEONETTI OR SIGNED BY HIM UNTIL AFTER LEONETTI WAS SENTENCED IN THE CRIMINAL MATTER.

THE WAIVER WAS THEREFORE "INVALID" FOR WAIVING THE CONFLICT IN THE CRIMINAL MATTER.

THE SUPREME COURT CONCLUDED THAT THE DISTRICT COURT ERRED BY DETERMINING THAT LEONETTI WAIVED ANY POTENTIAL CONFLICT THAT AROSE AS A RESULT OF THE SIMULTANEOUS REPRESENTATION OF MICHAEL LEONETTI AND DIANE.

You knew all along that James E. Guesman was Guilty but your choice was to cover-up for Guesman and the State. You knew that the victom signed a Police Report that she was never assaulted in anyway by me, however three (3) month's later as soon as she was fired from my Magazine for sexually assaulting my 11 year old daughter, she changes her story, and point's the finger at me.

There was NO PROBABLE CAUSE to arrest me, However this was the Perfect Opportunity to cover up the $250.000.00 thousand dollar claim that was being filed against the Las Vegas Police Dept. and the fear of being put on the front cover of my next issue.

On April 2,2004 at the hearing you were told by your Bailiff that James E. Guesman was conspiring to have me MURDERED in Prison or when I get out, you Instructed your Bailiff NOT! to Report the crime, you both had a duty, but you failed and committed a Class B Felony, Guesman had all the motive to carry out his plan. Once again you covered up for Guesman.

You knew that Guesman signed a Guilty Plea May 15,2001, you knew that Guesman was a PSYCHOPATH, Guesman Defruded myself and five (5) other Victims you knew and Leon Simion knew that Guesman was lying under oath and was not telling the truth, the evidence was right in front of you both, but you kept it quiet.

There were three (3) witness's on April 2,2004 that would of testified on the spot that they heard Guesman and Don Rux conspiring to have me murdered, but you did not bring those witness's on the stand, if that would of happened would of showed the court that all the criminal allegation's I made against Guesman were TRUE!.

This shows that you rather keep a innocent man in prison, then expose those that committed the crime. Your Job is to up-hold the law not break the law. You were told on the record on April 2,2004 that Judge Robert Gaston signed a ORDER on March 11,2004 that Guesman Committed " FRAUD" Rule 60 (b) in Family Court,

2.

DECEIT CORRUPTION COVER-UP

you Disregared the Evidence that was told to you.

    On September 10,2004 a motion was put into the court for the name of the Bailiff, so he could be brought into Court to testify as to what the three (3) witness's told him what Guesman and Rux were going to do. You Dined ever Motion that I put into the Court to keep this injustice quite. You did this to protect the truth from coming out, and for you to be exposed.

    There is enough evidence against you to take to the Grand Jury for an INDICTMENT, your Unconsciousable actions has put the District Attorney, Attorney General, Nevada Bar,and the Judicial Disiplinary Commission in a very Embarrassing Situation your Deliberate Disobedience has Jeopardized the Intergity of those that are thier to inforce the Law, your actions has put a dark cloud over all of them.

    You even jeopardized Judge Kathy Hardcastle she put herself back on my case just to save YOU! after she Disqualifies herself on October 15,2003.
I am sure that Mrs. Hardcastle can see now why her husband was to be Subpoenaed into Court to Testify, if Gerald Hardcastle would of known that Guesman was Representing me in a criminal case and Diane Leonetti in the Divorce, he NEVER would of signed the ORDER... Guesman made a fool out of him and abused his friendship, Guesman never thought that he would ever been cought, by Guesman doing what he did I lost all that I had.

    On April 4,2006, April 11,2006, April 25,2006, April 27,2006 May 18,2006, June 19,2007 and July 17,2007. Mr. Massinino P. Russello and Mr. Tony Earl was in the court room in my behalf asking why! I was not brought to court to plead my case, everytime that these men went to Court for me, you were very very Belligerent to them.

    There were two times that you told Mr. Russello that Judge Kathy HardCastle don't like me because of the way that I spoke to her, Mr. Russello will testify to what you said in Court.
The Public need to know that you been accused of a crime and you will not stand up to prove your innocent.

    You took an Oath, an Oath you can't Obey,
Cannon 3 (1) states;
    UNDER THE RULE, A JUDGE IS DISQUALIFIED WHENEVER THE JUDGE'S IMPARTIALITY MIGHT REASONABLE BE QUESTIONED.
    There is enough evidence under Frderal Law 42 U.S.C.S. 1985 & 1986 U.S.C.S. 241 & 242 plus NRS Rule 8. To put you in a Federal Prison for 10 years

For the sake of Justice and for the people that voted you in office step down from the bench and get the proper help you need, you have been accused of a breaking the law, now it is your turn to stand for what is right.

3.

MICHAEL LEONETTI

When you Speak the Truth you Declare Righteousness.
As Supreme Court Justice Rose said in the March 7,2006 ORDER Granting Mr. Leonetti's Petition Case No. 46369.
THE PROCEEDINGS AT ISSUE IN THIS WRITARE " TORTURED"

Judge Glass your actions were the cause of that Statement. You must be held Accountable by Law for the crimes you been accused of.

                          Cordially
                          Michael Leonetti #67009
                          Southern Desert Correctional Center
                          Post Office Box 208
                          Indian Springs, Nevada
                          89070-0208

certificate of mailing

I , Michael Leonetti, do hereby certify that on the 7th day of September 2007 I placed in a envelope, postage, preppaid, my letter to Judge Jackie Glass to Resign from the Bench and to turn herself in to the proper Authorites, to the Following addresses:

1. Clerk, U.S. District Court
   District Of Nevada
   Lloyd D. George / U.S. Courthouse
   333 Las Vegas, Blvd. South Room 1334
   Las Vegas, Nevada 89101
2. David Rogers, Esq.
   District Attorney of Nevada
   200 Lewis Ave. 3rd Floor
   Las Vegas, Nevada 89155
3. Attorney General
   Ms. Catherine Cortez Masto Esq.
   100 North Carson Street
   Carson City, Nevada 89701-4717
4. Judge Jackie Glass
   Eighth Judicial District Court
   Regional Justice Center
   200 Lewis Ave. 3rd Floor
   Las Vegas, Nevada 89155
5. Mr. James Tuftlan Esq.
   Clark County District Attorney
   200 Lewis Ave.
   Las Vegas, Nevada 89155
6. Judge Kathy A. HardCastle Chief Judge
   200 Lewis Ave. 3rd Floor
   Las Vegas, Nevada 89155
7. Judge Gerald HardCastle
   Family Court
   601 North Pecos Rd.
   Las Vegas, Nevada 89101
8. Massimino P. Russello
   2817 Nikki Terrace
   Henderson Nevada 89074

                          Respectfully Submitted
                          Michael Leonetti #67009

4.

DECEIT CORRUPTION COVER-UP

Michael Leonetti #67009
Southern Desert Correctional Center
Post Office Box 208 Indian Springs, Nevada
89070-0208
In Proper Person

UNITED STATES DISTRICT COURT

SOUTHERN DISTRICT OF NEVADA

MICHAEL LEONETTI,

Petitioner,

Vs:
THE STATE OF Nevada
Judge JACKIE GLASS
Attorney General, Ms. Catherine Cortez Masto
Deputy Attorney General, HEIDI
NEVADA BAR, David Clark

District Attorney, David Rogers Esq.
Nevada Commission on Judicial Discipline, David Sarnowski

Case Ro. 2:07-CV-0236-&JD-RJJ
District case No. C-169467 Judicial Comission No. 2005-13

MOTION FOR DEFAULT JUDGEMENT

COMES NOW Defendant, MICHAEL LEONETTI, before this Court, who now prays that this Court grant unto him this Motion for cause, and the relief sought unto him a finding unto him a judgement against the following parties for cause:

1. THE STATE OF NEVADA
2. JUDGE JACKIE GLASS
3•. ATTORNEY GENERAL, MS. CATHERINE CORTEZ MASTO ESQ.
4. DEPUTY ATTORNEY, HEIDIE. NAGEL ESQ.
5. NEVADA BAR, DAVID CLARK ESQ.
6. DISTRICT ATTORNEY, DAVID ROGERS ESQ.
7. NEVADA JUDICIAL COMMISSION, DAVID SARNOWSKI ESQ.

Defendant has filed a Motion to Compel on August 29, 2007 as of this date neither of the parties have filed a motion for extensions of time to file an answer to the criminal allegations of Premediated Fraud by James E. Guesman Esq., Perjury, Ethics Violation's, Federal Violation's, Judicial Conduct, Cannon Violation's, Conspiracy to Commit Murder,

I.

Michael Leonetti #67009
Southern Desert Correctional Center
Post Office Box 208
Indian Springs, Nevada 89070-0208
Attorney Pro Se

UNITED STATES DISTRICT COURT
DISTRICT OF NEVADA

MICHAEL LEONETTI,
    Petitioner,

Vs:

THE STATE OF NEVADA
1. JUDGE JACKIE GLASS
2. ATTORNEY GENERAL MS. CATHERINE CORTEZ MASTO
3. CHIEF JUDGE KATHY HARDCASTLE
4. NEVADA DISTRICT ATTORNEY DAVID ROGERS
    Respondents,

Case No. 2:07-cv-0236-KJD-RJJ
District Case No. C-169467
Complaint No. 2005-13

MOTION FOR DEFAULT JUDGEMENT

    COMES NOW, MICHAEL LEONETTI, before this federal court, who now prays that this court grant unto him this motion for cause and relief sought unto him a finding of judgement against the parties for cause.

    The Petitioner filed a motion on November 7,2007 to the federal court to seek Redress and federal violations under 18 U.S.C. § 241 & 242 against the Respondents. The were to were to respond by November 25,2007 as of this date neither parties have filed any motions for extensions of time to file an answer to the Criminal and Federal Violations the Respondents are accused of, Premeditated Fraud, Perjury, Ethics Violations, Federal Violations, Conspiracy to Commit Murder and Malicious Prosecution.

    IT IS A FEDERAL CRIME TO CONSPIRE FOR THE PURPOSE OF "IMPEDING" "HINDERING" "OBSTRUCTING" OR "DEFEATING" THE DUE COURSE OF JUSTICE.

2.

DECEIT CORRUPTION COVER-UP

DATED THIS 26th DAY OF SEPTEMBER 2007

Respectfully Submitted

#67009

Michael Leonetti
Southern Desert Correctional Center Post Office Box 208
Indian Springs, Nevada 89070-0208
Attorney Pro Se

MICHAEL LEONETTI

Michael Leonetti #67009
Southern Desert Correctional Center
Post Office Box 208
Indian Springs, Nevada 89070-0208
Attorney In Proper Person

2008 FEB 13 P 3:47

UNITED STATES DISTRICT COURT
DISTRICT OF NEVADA

MICHAEL LEONETTI,

    Petitioner,

VS:

THE STATE OF NEVADA,

    Respondents,

Case. No. 2:07-cv-0236-KJD-RJJ

District Case No. C-169467

Complaint No. 2005-13

Pursuant to F.R.C.P. 55 (a) (b) (2) (a)

REAL PARTY INTEREST
1. **JUDGE JACKIE GLASS**
2. **Attorney General Ms. Catherine Cortez Masto**
3. **CHIEF JUDGE KATHY HARDCASTLE**
4. **DAVID ROGERS, NEVADA DISTRICT ATTORNEY**

NOTICE OF MOTION
F.R.C.P. 55

YOU WILL PLEASE TAKE NOTICE, THAT THIS FEDERAL COURT GRANT UNTO THE PETITIONER MICHAEL LEONETTI, THIS MOTION FOR CAUSE AND RELIEF UNTO HIM A FINDING OF JUDGEMENT OF CONVICTION AGAINST THE RESPONDENTS FOR CAUSE.

WILL COME ON FOR HEARING BEFORE THE ABOVE-ENTITLED COURT ON THE ____ DAY OF _____, 2008 AT THE HOUR OF ____ O'CLOCK ____.M. IN DEPT. _____, OF SAID COURT.

DATED THIS 11 DAY OF February, 2008

By: _____
Michael Leonetti #67009
Southern Desert Correctional Center
Post Office Box 208
Indian Springs, Nevada 89070-0208
Attorney Proper Person

1.

DECEIT CORRUPTION COVER-UP

Michael Leonetti #67009
Southern Desert Correctional Center
Post Office Box 208 Indian Springs, Nevada
89070-0208
In Proper Person

UNITED STATES DISTRICT COURT 2007 SEP 28p /: 10

SOUTHERN DISTRICT OF NEVADA

MICHAEL LEONETTI,

Petitioner,

Vs:
THE STATE OF Nevada

Judge JACKIE GLASS

Attorney General, Ms. Catherine Cortez Masto
Deputy Attorney General, HEIDI

NEVADA BAR, David Clark

District Attorney, David Rogers Esq.
Nevada Commission on Judicial Discipline, David Sarnowski

Case Ro. 2:07-CV-0236-&JD-RJJ

District case No. C-169467 Judicial Comission No. 2005-13

MOTION FOR DEFAULT JUDGEMENT

COMES NOW Defendant, MICHAEL LEONETTI, before this Court, who now prays that this Court grant unto him this Motion for cause, and the relief sought unto him a finding unto him a judgement against the following parties for cause:

1. THE STATE OF NEVADA
2. JUDGE JACKIE GLASS
3•. ATTORNEY GENERAL, MS. CATHERINE CORTEZ MASTO ESQ.
4. DEPUTY ATTORNEY, HEIDIE. NAGEL ESQ.
5. NEVADA BAR, DAVID CLARK ESQ.
6. DISTRICT ATTORNEY, DAVID ROGERS ESQ.
7. NEVADA JUDICIAL COMMISSION, DAVID SARNOWSKI ESQ.

Defendant has filed a Motion to Compel on August 29, 2007 as of this date neither of the parties have filed a motion for extensions of time to file an answer to the criminal allegations of Premediated Fraud by James E. Guesman Esq., Perjury, Ethics Violation's, Federal Violation's, Judicial Conduct, Cannon Violation's, Conspiracy to Commit Murder,

I.

Therefore the Petitioner now moves this Federal Court to GRANT unto the Petitioner a Judgement of Default based upon the parties listed in this Motion and for the following:

D.C.R. 13 (3) F.R.C.P. 55 (a) (b) (2) (a) SO PROVIDES THAT A PARTY WHO HAS BEEN SERVED A MOTION AND OR PLEADINGS SHALL FILE A RESPONSE AND OR OPPOSITION WITHIN TEN (10) DAYS OF RECEIT. FAILURE TO DO SO, THE RESPONDENT IS GRANTING UNTO THE COURT THE RIGHT TO GRANT UNTO THE MOVING PARTY THE MOTION BASED UPON IMPLIED CONSENT, AS THE RESPONDENT IS ADMITTING THE MOTION IS BOTH MERITORIOUS AND PROPER AND UNDEFENDABLE.

Therefore based upon the actions of the Respondents that have been accused of a federal crime of a criminal nature, the Petitioner Michael Leonetti moves this Honorable Court for a Judgement in his favor and to GRANT the following Relief:

1. **FOR THIS COURT TO SANCTION THE PARTIES IN THIS MOTION TO THE MAXIMUM PENALTIES ALLOWABLE UNDER LAW. TO ENFORCE FEDERAL LAW 18 U.S.C. § 241 & 242 AND SENTENCE THE RESPONDENTS NO LESS THEN TEN (10) YEARS IN A FEDERAL PRISON FOR THE RESPONDENTS TO BE IMPEACHED FROM PUBLIC OFFICE ALSO DISBARRED AND NEVER TO PRACTICE LAW AGAIN IN ANY STATE IN THIS COUNTRY. THIS ALSO INCLUDES,**

MR. JAMES E. GUESMAN ESQ. BAR NO. 1610 & MR. DONALD W. RUX.

CONCLUSION

The Respondents, Judge Jackie Glass, Attorney General Ms. Catherine Cortez Masto, Chief Judge Kathy Hardcastle, David Rogers, Nevada District Attorney, James E. Guesman Esq. and Donald Rux. What was done to Mr. Leonetti by these people were Disgraceful, what was done to the Petitioner went against all that Justice and the United States stands for, and the laws their Compelled to follow.

The Respondents have displayed their DESPICABLE DISOBEDIENCE in up holding the Laws they took an Oath to Obey. There obstinate behavior showed they refused to Obey the Law, The Respondents actions are selfsufficient that the law is not

DECEIT CORRUPTION COVER-UP

about GUILT or INNOCENCE, but it is about POWER and the right to go against the laws they MUST! abide by without hesitation. Their behavior proves their above the law and they believe they have a right to destroy as many lives with no Conscience. INNOCENCE, ETHICS, CANNON LAW, MORAL INTEGRITY is IRRELEVANT.

The Respondents never at any time answered any of the Motions that were filed with the Federal Court. The Respondents know the Petitioners Claims and Criminal allegations are Meritorious Proper and Undefendable.

DATED THIS 11th DAY of FEBRUARY 2008

Respectfully submitted;

By: _____
Michael Leonetti #67009
Southern Desert Correctional Center
Post Office Box 208
Indian Springs, Nevada 89070-0208
Attorney Proper Person

/////
/////
/////

4.

A hand-written pleading was filed with the Supreme Court of Nevada, Case No. 54624, on November 2, 2009. The Court accepted the hand-written draft and allowed it to be entered onto the docket. "On October 24, 2009, Appellant (Michael Leonetti) was requested to see investigator Knoff from S.D.C.C. A letter was sent from outside the S.D.C.C. to Warden Brian Williams from an anonymous party stating: Due to the nature of the appellant's crime it would be only a matter of time that Michael Leonetti would be murdered. This judicial notice is based upon the following evidence submitted to the Court and documents in the file of Appellant at S.D.C.C." The letter provides the details of the conspiracy to have Michael assassinated in prison. There are attachments detailing his allegations with the pleading ending as follows: "Till this very day the Attorney General refused to uphold N.R.S. 228.175 and never once investigated the crimes...."

To no avail, none of the motions Michael sent to court received action. Judges recused themselves, no one wanted to touch the allegations, no one was going to point fingers of any wrong doing. *What is amazing about this fact that 11 judges recused themselves in this case. There is not another case in history whereby eleven judges recused themselves.*

Michael remained in prison until his sentence was completed. He received letters recognizing the pleadings but nothing that would stir anyone to action.

He never stopped fighting. His case finally reached the Supreme Court 9th Circuit. It was captioned: Michael

Leonetti vs. Brian Williams and Attorney General of the State of Nevada. That was an answer to Michael's begging the court allowing his case be dismissed and set him free. It was filled with legal jargon all very convincing and written by seasoned lawyers. The problem was that it was too convincing and the Court upheld the Respondent's Answer, siding with the Brian Williams (respondents).

Michael fought back drafting another appeal listing a myriad of errors made by the Court but again that appeal wasn't given credence, and he lost the appeal.

Life in prison dragged on from day to day as he woke each morning in a tiny jail cell, was released into the yard for exercise and socialization, attended classes, ate meals, and slept. A dull, monotonous existence for a man who had given so much to so many. The one person he could depend on was his mother, the letters arrived each and every day. A sign that he was loved by someone.

There was a man Michael had befriended when he was a chef in Las Vegas. Massie was a waiter and the two struck up a close and long friendship. Michael wrote to him and explained where he was spending his time and Massie came each month to visit his dear friend. For eight years he kept the vigil, each month arriving at the same time and spending a couple hours of comradery. When it was time to part, they would hug and Michael would observe his friend walking through the visitor's door. After each visit, the guards took Michael to a small private room at the edge of the visiting room. Two guards would take over the strip search, one commanded Michael to remove all his clothes, the other put on latex gloves and began a thorough body search, commencing with the top of his head (which was bald), they pried open his mouth, examined his genitals, and told him to bend over so they could examine his anus.

Humiliation with a touch of sadomasochism was how Michael ended each visit. Drugs, the guards were searching for drugs or anything else that was left behind which could be construed as illegal paraphernalia. One guard would do the physical exam and the other would serve as the voyeur, observing the examination. It would be understandable if many inmates refused to see visitors based upon the punishment of a strip search after each interaction. To be put through a strip search each time a spouse, a friend, an attorney, a member of the clergy, a relative came to visit, was a severe punishment. Michael, like his fellow inmates, bit their lip and suffered through the disgusting examination. He was always clean.

Life in prison was not only miserable but a never-ending minefield of violence and revenge. An example of such an incidence: Michael was in the law library working with an inmate on his case. A female caseworker was also in the library and Michael's friend wanted her to notice him. He tried to get her attention, maybe she would assist him, or see him on a visit or better, maybe the caseworker would have sex with him. Hallucinating wildly as the caseworker sat quietly reading through cases, he approached her and she instantly rebuffed his advances. Michael was watching the scene and when his friend returned to the table, he was agitated and angry. Embarrassed, Michael's friend decided to take out his anger on Michael. Writing a love letter, filled with sexual connotation, he signed it; Michael Leonetti.

At daylight the following morning, Michael was roused out of his top bunk by several guards. They threw him down on the floor, handcuffed him, placed the heel of a shoe at his throat and announced he was going back to the hole. Clueless, he had no choice but to do as he was told. Two days later, he was notified what had happened, a fellow inmate had signed Michael's name to the sexually filled note to the caseworker. Back in black hell, he demanded a graphologist, who could easily discern that the signature on the note was forged. After the eight weeks had ended, his demand was granted. It was not Michael's signature but the damage had been done, he had suffered, yet again. The Warden, Sheryl Foster, had no time or inclination to give Michael an opportunity to prove himself. Prison was not a democratic place where one had a chance at speaking the truth, it was an autocracy, run solely by the Warden. Only one voice was heard, only one voice set the rules.

The situations Michael witnessed while in the confines of prison were unlike anything in free society. There was a pecking order of power with the Warden situated at the very top. All power trickled down to the lowest, weakest human sleeping in the cells. Inmates used their power over each other in situations as just described. Addressing sexual behavior exploitation: the toughest inmates implemented their prowess over the weaklings. They never touched Michael, he always responded with "NO!" and they stayed away. He also sported a fit strong body that was embellished with pumped up muscles. Tough, the sexual predators stayed away. One evening, before lock-up, he observed four overweight men walk into a cell and proceed to rape a frail older man. It was obscene, leaving the man lying on the floor, lifeless and near death. No one called for help, they turned away. Tattle tailing in prison was not part of the culture. Turning a blind eye was how inmates survived unscathed by sexual predators.

The weakest inmates were further abused by becoming slaves to the stronger more powerful men; they were forced to wash their clothes, clean toilets, make their beds and do whatever whim suited the powerful inmates. An inmate nicknamed Big Pretty, an ex-football player, was tall, heavy and completely muscle bound; he intimidated most of the prisoners just by his sheer size. When he wanted something, he got it and it was usually in the form of sex. Michael watched him walk into man's cell, punch him out, and rape the unconscious man. Later the victim woke up and found his pants and underwear around his ankles wondering what the hell had happened.

Life in prison was not a reflection of the real world, it was surreal with ugly unfair evil people running and ruling the activity of its inhabitants. *They took away my freedom but not my talent, not my ability to sing and perform, not my love for my mother and not my ability to continue fighting my case. I will have all of this until I take my last breath.*

There was a fine line between sanity and insanity. So much that occurred inside the walls of Indian Springs reflected insanity. Fear ran rampant, it was a tool used to control the population. Most of the time it worked, the cellmates were usually complacent, and calm but the instances that took away lives, were unforgettable and frightening. Each day within the walls of the correctional institution could only be defined as agonizing especially when one was sent there as an innocent man. Hope was an attribute Michael rarely allowed himself to feel, what he had to rely on was time, ticking off each day on the calendar when he would leave, an alive breathing human being.

Chapter 16

FREEDOM ARRIVED

On March 12, 2012, a guard arrived at Michael's cell, walked him to a small room, provided a change of clothing and handed him $200.00 in cash. Surprised, the guard explained when cash was sent to the inmates, some of the money was withheld in a bank account for this very moment. Another guard arrived and escorted him to the entrance gate turned the key and Michael walked out of the prison. He dropped down on his knees and kissed the gravel. Looking up at the clear March sky, his eyes sprouted tears of joy, at long last, he had his freedom.

"Hey Michael," yelled a strange voice. He scanned the parking lot and saw a man waving his arm. "I am your ride to the airport." Without hesitating, Michael jogged to the car, opened the door and took a seat. "Your friend arranged for me to give you a ride."

Michael shook his hand offered a genuine thank you and rolled down the window of the car, breathing in air, fresh, free, cool air. Ahhhh, it felt great. The driver handed Michael a one-way ticket to Las Vegas and $500, "Complements of your friend Tommy Powers," he added. The short drive to the airport was the best road trip Michael had experienced in over a decade. Parking the car, the driver guided Michael into the small airport, and took him for breakfast. They ordered a substantial meal and the driver handed Michael the phone. His first call, and only call was to his mom. Tears flooded down his face as he told her he was out of prison and a free man. "I'll call you with my address when I get settled."

"It's gotta be hard," said the driver. "I did time, not as much as you, but it was hell. I have been on the straight and narrow and I know that is how you will live your life."

When the food arrived Michael ate voraciously, the first decent meal in twelve years. Savoring every bite, he guzzled down the rich coffee and thanked the driver.

"Good luck," said the driver as he walked back to his car and Michael strolled to the gate. He laughed to himself when he cleared security, all he had was the clothing on his back and a few dollars in his pocket. At fifty-nine, he was beginning another chapter in his life. He took a window seat so he had an unobstructed view of the cloudless sky. At that moment he reflected on his life. He was completely alone. For the first time in his entire life he was without another human being, no one to watch over him, no one to give a hug or kiss, there was just, no one, at all.

The few dollars in his pocket would hardly make it through a day or two. He had to conjure up a plan and quickly, the flight from Reno to Las Vegas was barely an hour. Shortly, he would land, foregoing the luggage carousel, and emerge from the airport with no place to go, no one to meet, no job, no money, no place to sleep, a scary situation for a fifty-nine-year-old man. The weight of imprisonment was an albatross clinging around his neck. He knew there would be plenty of rough days ahead but he was determined to take back all that had been taken away. He would plod ahead with endless motions to the courts but now, as a free man he had to consider managing everyday life.

Walking towards the exit Michael saw a familiar face. Standing erect, in a pristine white shirt and pressed black pants, Massie was waving and calling out, "Michael." Smiling he lunged towards his friend, gave him a big hug and sprouted his usual round of tears, at least that time, the tears were joyful. Massie knew Michael had nothing and wanted to assist a great friend get back on his feet. The first words out of his mouth, "You will come and live with me until you get yourself together. It may not be easy, but I promise to help you get back on track and pick up your life." Michael's response was simply to keep on crying. So overcome by Massie's generosity, he couldn't get the words out. A short drive to Henderson and Michael arrived at his new (temporary) home. Turning to Massie he said, "Thank you, I'll never forget what you are doing for me."

"Seeing how you don't have to unpack," he chuckled, "How about a drink?" He poured a gin for himself and a large glass of wine for Michael.

He smelled the wine, and took a hearty gulp, it was like nectar from the gods. It did the trick and he began to relax.

They chatted for a while and later, Massie grabbed a pen and paper, "We need to get you organized. Let's make a list of what needs to be done."

Michael perked up, "I need a job, I have to have some money."

"Check," said Massie. "My friend has a construction company and he is going to give you a job. It is hard labor, but it's a start and pays ten bucks an hour."

"For a man that just spent twelve years in prison, it sounds like heaven. I would be absolutely happy to take the job. I know I am starting over, starting from the bottom, but at least there is only one way, and that is up."

Massie continued on with the list, "a driver's license, a bank account, a credit card, cell phone, clothing, a…."

"Stop!" said Michael, "too much." They carried their drinks to the backyard and turned on some music. At first Michael began to hum and then he belted out the tune. He cried, (anything and everything made him cry), and smiled. Staring up at the sky, he mumbled, *maybe God has not forsaken me, maybe God is testing me. Saying, hey Michael, how much can you take? How strong can you be?*

That night and for the entire time he remained in Massie's home, Michael prepared dinner. He cleaned the home, did the laundry, made the beds, landscaped the backyard and washed the car. Thankful for the friendship and a place to stay, he welcomed the work. Every morning Massie would drop Michael at the worksite and pick him up at the end of the day. The construction job was as tough as Massie had promised, digging ditches, pouring cement, carrying large pieces of lumber and pounding boards. When he would look up at the sky, he would remember he was a free man and had control over his life. At the end of each week, he was paid in cash and he stuffed it away in his pocket. Returning to his bedroom, he placed his earnings into a small paper bag. He spent nothing, yet he needed everything.

Massie had a petulance for contemporary clothing and every closet was stuffed with clothes. Although not a perfect fit, he gave Michael a small collection of clothing, certainly good enough to wear to the construction job. Early Saturday morning, they drove to a discount store and Michael spent part of his pay on a pair of shoes, underwear, and toiletries. When they returned home, he was filled with pride as he opened the shoe box and laced up his first purchase.

Later, Massie sat down and handed Michael a list of do's and dont's. Even though the two men were friends, neither had lived together. It became readily apparent that Massie had an anal-retentive personality and was obsessed with things being done in an exact manner. Michael had been living that way for twelve years and quickly arrived at the conclusion he needed to move out as soon as possible but on his meager salary he would have to be patient. Checking the cash in the paper bag, he realized it would take six months to save the money he needed to rent an apartment. Biting his lip, he smiled, took the list, two-hundred items long, and promised to abide by Massie's house rules.

Out of society for a dozen years there were a lot of things he had to learn. Co-workers advised him on where he should purchase a cell phone and then tutored him in how to use it. He began surfing the web and called the Jockey Club, a place he had worked almost two decades prior, selling time shares. Making an appointment with the owners, Richard Braglia and Al Rodriguez, Michael dressed in the best outfit Massie had given him, took a bus and rode down to the strip. Nervous, he was worried the albatross wound around his neck would prohibit the owners from re-hiring him. Strutting into the wooden paneled executive suite, the two men rose, shook Michael's hand, offered him a cup of coffee and discussed the job, his past performance and his future. When the short meeting was over, they hired Michael to be the man on the street enticing tourists to view the timeshare video which eventually led to a purchase.

Aware of Michael's circumstance, Richard lent their newest employee a car until he got on his feet. They discussed the details of the job, where he would be situated, the hours, and the salary.

The very next day, Sunday, he drove to the strip, took his position in front of Planet Hollywood and began hustling timeshares. He was a bull, tough, tenacious, and bold. With years of experience under his belt, it came flooding back. At the end of the day, he had escorted a dozen prospects in to view the video presentation. He never took a day off. Seven days a week he stood in front of one casino or another, bringing in prospects. Within a couple of months, he was able to move out of Massie's home and into a modest apartment close to the strip. Purchasing a car was still somewhere in the horizon, but he had nice new shoes on his feet, clean suits and shirts and money in the bank. Day by day, he rose, determined to make more money than the day before. Keeping meticulous records, his goal was to out sell the week before. True, the business was seasonal, he set realistic sights and goals. One day at a time became his moto.

Sunday evening, he returned to the apartment, sweat was dripping from every pore in his body. The outside temperature was near one-hundred degrees but that didn't deter him from selling the timeshares. He could endure the worst heat, anything, short of death, was a step up from the hell he had endured for the last twelve years. It was all level of comparison, and for Michael standing under the scorching summer heat, baking in desert temperatures, was a piece of cake. HE WAS FREE!!!!!

Stripping off the three-piece suit, he turned the shower on to a tepid temperature and stood for a half-hour cooling off his body. Attuned to prison life, he had yet to learn to relax and enjoy the feeling of the water gushing against his skin. Always in fear someone would jump him unexpectedly, his guard was up even inside his small private shower. There were many nights when he woke in the middle of the night dripping in sweat; he thought he was still sleeping on the thin cot inside his cell. Leaving the physical confines of prison didn't fully transfer to living in the free world. His memory, rampart with fear and the horrors of incarceration, still raged through his mind. It was as if his head was filled with cobwebs of years of prison life and he was unable to shred them from his mind.

While his incessant crying had finally tapered off, there were many moments when he felt sorry for himself and the conspiracy on his life. Duped into a prison sentence, he sometimes felt stupid. He would shake those depressing thoughts out of his mind and remember the talents God had given him; things could have been a lot worse. He could have died, he had read the letter from the two witnesses, he knew there was a plot to have him killed behind bars. God was watching out for Michael and that never took place.

There he stood, underneath the showerhead very much alive! Toweling off, he brushed off the steam on the mirror and saw a reflection of a decently handsome guy, with an unlined face, muscular body and a voice that had not forsaken him during the last twelve years. He had a lot to be thankful for. Mentally he listed all his blessings, dressed for work and walked out the door. It was another scorching day underneath the desert sun, but he was armed with four frozen bottles of water, a smile and an obsession to make money. His company moved him to different casinos, sometimes he was at the Bellagio, or Planet Hollywood, or downtown on Fremont Street. Las Vegas Boulevard was teeming with pedestrian traffic, there was always a guarantee that throngs of tourists would be passing by as he hustled the timeshare concept.

He met, literally, thousands of people and held thousands of conversations, all to lure prospects into the virtues of owning a timeshare. For three years, seven days a week, he worked relentlessly, never taking a day off. Saving every dime, except on the bare necessities of living, he continued to view the docket as his case inched through the State Court into the Federal District Court. If he needed money to prove his innocence, he would have it when the time arrived. Safely tucked in a bank account, he rarely made withdraws. He had no safety net except himself and that would mean creating a nest egg.

Las Vegas was known for hosting conventions. The timeshare convention was in the near horizon and his boss invited him to represent the company and run the booth. If anyone could draw attention, it would be Michael, he was the number one seller in the company. Flattered, he went out of his way to make sure the booth was set up properly, stocked with drinks, snacks and a bevy of company logo give-away items. Printing additional business cards, he was prepared for the mass surge of potential buyers. Dressed in a linen cream-colored suit, thin linen shirt, dark brown Oxfords, he looked the part of wealthy tourist seeking a home in Las Vegas, or other properties owned by the parent company. That was his first convention. Nervous, he needed to prove himself and to his boss that he could sell his heart out from the moment the doors opened until the last customer left the convention center.

Gulping down some coffee, he was armed for the influx of thousands flooding the convention floor. Pamphlets in hand, he surreptitiously cajoled prospects into his booth and sold them on the virtues of his timeshare company. Sometimes he became so hyped, he sang and drew small clusters of curious tourists. A tall handsome man was passing by and turned his head towards the singer.

"Michael, Michael Leonetti" he shouted, "Is that you? Because I sure recognize that voice."

They hugged, ignoring the crowd. Tears of joy sputtered down Michael's eyes. "Pete, it has been so long. So great to see you," cried Michael.

"Look, I see you are busy. I'll come back at the end of the day and we can reminisce."

Pete Allman had befriended Michael when he began performing in Las Vegas. Pete was a performer who had his own television variety show, *Las Vegas Tonight*, which provided local performers a platform to promote their talent. Michael was one of the guests who had a substantial following. When Pete announced the line-up of upcoming shows he noticed an up-tick in viewership when Leonetti sang. "Not only was Michael a great singer but he had a beautiful soul and knew how to reach the audience at home. He loved the camera and the camera loved him."

Pete had kept abreast of Michael's tragedy but they had not communicated until that very day at the convention. "None of his singing talent was lost, but I could see he had put up a lot of walls. He had been so badly burned he was afraid to trust anyone, especially women."

As for Pete, he had spent the last twelve years expanding his television show into a vast production empire, producing CMX Sports and Entertainment, movies and other television shows. Known as a journalist, he wrote for the *Las Vegas Magazine*, and hosted a talk show with "A" list celebrities. One of his current enterprises, introduced in 2018, was OCN Christian network. "I want to put Michael on my show. What he went through and the hell he endured. Yet, he inspired thousands of men with his biblical plays. He brought the worst of mankind closer to God, and without God the human soul is void. I want the world to see what my friend has done. Maybe it was God's mission to test Michael, to see how much he could endure but he never gave up believing."

Later that evening, after a grueling day on his feet, Michael met Pete for dinner. They talked for hours, so much to catch up on, so much time lost.

"Can you try not to cry," said Pete.

"It's hard not to. You know what they called me in prison? 'Crying Mike.' I couldn't help myself, I literally cried a river of tears. Thanks Pete for being my friend. As you can guess almost everyone else abandoned me."

"Hell, friend, I know damn well you didn't do it, the whole thing was a set-up, a conspiracy. In the end God will punish those evil people who did this to you. But from the looks of things, prison didn't destroy your voice, nor your physique. You still have muscles. For me, well I kind of let that go by the wayside."

When the steaks arrived, Pete observed his friend digging into the food as if it were his first meal. He was keenly aware Michael had lost all his assets and was starting over at age sixty. An idea sprouted in his mind, "You still cooking? Boy do I remember all those fantastic parties at your home and all those delicious dishes. To this day, I have never eaten better Italian food."

"I remember every recipe, it's still up here," Michael responded, as he used his index finger pointing to his brain. "Along with so many other things, including sex, I miss cooking but I know how to prepare every dish." Unable to keep his emotions under control, tears formed at the corners of his eyes, "Gosh I miss chopping garlic," he laughed, a euphemism for remaining celibate.

The plate, wiped clean, Pete called the waiter over and ordered his old friend another steak. Michael would never forget the kindness Pete showed him.

Pete's offer to host a cooking show was the beginning of Michael's return to the world of performing. His first thought was to call him mom, who would be overcome with joy when she heard the news.

Chapter 17

After weeks of preparations, the first production aired. With little fanfare, the small initial audience received the half-hour show well and the critics deemed it an excellent slant on the typical variety program. Showcasing the best the city had to offer, it did what it was intended to do; entertain. With each episode, the audience grew larger, guaranteeing the sponsorship and the continuation.

Michael never gave up his timeshare job. In spite of the television and later, a radio show, he maintained his obsession for making money. Never putting all his eggs in one basket, he understood the world of entertaining and what was great one day could be gone the next. Thus, on the weekends, when tourists thronged Las Vegas Boulevard, he was in front of the casinos procuring potential timeshare buyers. Always in a well-tailored suit, his good looks and congenial voice immediately attracted pedestrians. Placing a pamphlet into the palm of their hands, he would look them squarely in the eye, convincing them he was about to offer them a dream of a lifetime, a perpetual vacation. Shortly after capturing their attention, he piqued their interest, and pried open their pocket books. He was still the number one salesperson even though he had trimmed back hours.

The job was the one piece of security he could cling onto. The company loved him and religiously made direct deposits into his checking account; they never short-changed his commissions, nor bickered over a customer. The company was always satisfied with Michael's performance and he was content with the constant inflow of income. After losing twelve years of income and all the wealth from his twenty-five years of marriage, he had a lot of catching up to do. The timeshare job slowly increased his savings, allowing him to purchase a townhome. The one asset that was solely in his name. It was demanding work, standing under the scorching sun for hours at a time, but after what he had endured in prison, to him, it was a walk in the park.

Pouring himself a glass of red wine, he opened the refrigerator, collected ingredients for a simple meal for one, chopped some sweet onions, tossed a salad, roasted sausages, boiled pasta and plunked himself down on his new sofa and turned on his new flat screen television. After watching the news, he cleaned the kitchen and returned to the living room. Alone, he felt himself slip into a feel-sorry, depressed mode. *No,* the other side of his brain responded, *you are not going to sit in your new home, that is completely yours and yours alone and wallow in self-pity. Pick yourself up and go for a walk.*

In the clarity of the crisp evening air, he walked purposefully, although where, he wasn't sure. His mind wasn't in the decision-making mood, but he knew there was a lot of unfinished business in his life. The fight in Federal Court weighed heavily on his mind. He had received updates every so often from the appointed public defender, but years later, nothing definitive had been ordered.

And then there was his family, he missed them so much. That problem could and would easily be resolved the following morning. He would invite his mom and son for another visit. After building up a sweat, he returned home, took a shower, and fell soundly asleep.

It felt like an eternity had passed since he hugged his mom and son. Dolores had aged and so had Michael Junior, who was sporting a cane and walking with an unsteady gait. At the airport, they took the elevator down one level, retrieved their luggage and walked into the parking lot. Michael placed the bags into the trunk, flipped on the air-conditioning and drove them to his new home. Still thin, Dolores appeared frail, but from her animated conversation, her mind was still intact. She was proud of her son, and prouder of her grandson, (whom she had raised since infancy). Michael Jr spread out in the backseat while his dad pointed out the new casinos dotting the Strip.

"Wow," he shouted, "Grandma just look at those huge places. Dad, do you sing in those places?"

"No, but I still do sing. How about I take you out tomorrow night and you can watch me perform while you dine on some authentic Italian food? The big casinos have done away with lounge acts and the showrooms attract only the A-list performers. I perform in the local restaurants and theatres. For me, I get the same thrill out of singing for a hundred people as for a thousand people, but as you can guess, the money isn't there. Performing has become my second career but at least I can still do what I love and do it well enough that I am booked most every weekend."

Slowly creeping northbound on the Strip, Michael pointed out more new sites, made a left turn and another ten minutes they arrived at his townhome. Parking the car, he opened the passenger doors, grabbed the two pieces of luggage and unlocked the front door. The smell of a new freshly painted home along with the large pot of sauce simmering on top of the stove wafted in the air as Dolores and Michael Jr walked through the front door.

"Dad you cooked us a pot of sauce? It smells just like Grandma's," said Michael Jr.

"Your dad was the one grandchild who inherited the cooking talents from your great grandmother. Michael, can you show your son the spoon?"

Obeying his mom, Michael slid open a utensil drawer and extracted a stained wooden spoon.

"This is magic, it has stirred thousands of pots of homemade sauce. When your great grandma made her last pot of sauce, she called me into her kitchen, handed me this spoon and told me I was responsible for continuing the family traditions. I would be known as the cook, and it was up to me to pass on the tradition to my kids. Life hasn't treated me so good in that area, so I did the next best thing. I co-hosted a variety show, I was Chef Michael and cooked for an audience of thousands each week. Every episode has been taped and can be viewed on the internet. After dinner, I'll show you the websites and you can see your dad cook the family recipes. Those recipes, once guarded in my memory, are now available for all to see. I let the cat out of the bag and the secrets to the Leonetti's claim to fame."

After a long nap, Dolores and Michael Jr joined Michael in the kitchen. The table was set and dinner was ready to eat. Pouring three glasses of wine, they toasted each other and dug into a sumptuous meal. Michael dispensed with soup, in the desert heat no one wanted to begin with a steaming bowl of minestrone. Instead, he placed a large crispy salad onto the table with a loaf of garlic bread and a bowl of marinated cold vegetables. Removing the platter, he replaced it with another filled with filet steaks, grilled to perfection, a side of roasted broccoli rabe, and stuffed portabella mushrooms.

"Dad, this food is so great, you should open a restaurant," piped up his son.

"I agree," said Dolores. "It's one thing to watch you on television but quite another to actually eat your food."

"I have thought about it," said Michael, "But that takes a lot of money and I'm not quite there yet. We all have our dreams and when the time is right, I hope to make that happen."

They sat around the table for hours, talking, reminiscing, laughing, crying and remembering a lifetime of family traditions. Upon reflection, life back in Philadelphia seemed simple, with less stress, and predictability. People were more transparent, honest, forthright, with a stronger link to religious beliefs. In many ways, life in Sin City, was the wild west, where sense of right and wrong was resolved in unconventional manners, and life wasn't so simple, so cut and dried. It seemed as though everybody and everything was complicated, life revolved around gray areas, not so much in black and white.

Dolores never mentioned prison, if her son wanted to talk about his experiences she would be receptive, but she had no intention of unearthing twelve hideous, wasted years of his life in futile conversation.

Michael opened his computer, pressed a few keys and up popped the website displaying him cooking, singing and conversing. "That should keep you two busy for a while," he laughed.

Early the next morning, he woke, brewed a pot of coffee, kissed his family good bye and headed to an abbreviated day of work. Returning early in the afternoon, he found his family seated outside on the small patio snoozing away. The time zone change had tuckered them out.

"How about lunch?" Michael yelled.

Dolores and Michael Jr's eyes flashed open. "I could eat," they said in unison. (Too much together time).

"Great because I have planned a fantastic meal for you," said Michael. "Tonight I am going to take you to a wonderful restaurant and you are going to watch me sing while you enjoy some really delicious pasta and wine."

"So, what's for lunch?"

Michael pulled a couple of pans from the cabinet, chopped some fresh garlic and parsley and tossed it into a pan with a generous layer of virgin olive oil. Twenty minutes later, they were devouring a huge bowl of fettuccine layered with huge pink prawns, fresh spinach and sundried tomatoes.

"We gotta have some wine," insisted Michael, "You are on vacation."

Grabbing three glasses and a chilled bottle of Chianti, he poured the wine and they toasted each other's good health.

"Dad, if I ate like this every day, I would be very fat. No one in our family was fat. Didn't you eat like this when you were a kid?"

Come to think of it you are right. We ate like this most every day and I can't recall one heavy relative. I think we walked a lot and never ate fast food. I don't eat like this every day, I save my traditional recipes for guests and lately, there hasn't been too many of them."

Dolores observed her son's face drop, she understood he was alluding to his years in prison and how most of his friends had deserted him when he finally emerged as a free man. Starting over at the age of fifty-nine, took a lot of energy, tenacity and gumption. Letting down her guard and caving into his nightmare wouldn't help him, she needed to be strong, like all those letters she wrote for twelve years. Gathering a smile, she picked up the bottle of wine, replenished the glasses until the last drop had been drained. Dolores insisted on cleaning the dishes while her son took a well-deserved nap. Michael Jr joined him outside and in the middle of their conversation, both men fell asleep. That's what happens when drinking wine, eating a huge lunch and sitting in the warm desert sun: a guaranteed recipe for an afternoon nap.

Grabbing his playlist, Michael announced it was time to leave for his gig. They piled into his roomy car and drove fifteen minutes to the venue. Michael loved the place. The main entrance was split, to the right was an expansive Italian deli packed with cured meat, pastas of every variety, freshly baked breads, veal (almost impossible to find in Las Vegas), red meats, frozen seafoods and a buffet of prepared foods. To the left was a narrow horseshoe shaped oak bar, cocktail tables and further back were dozens of tables, draped in white linens, prepared for the onslaught of diners. One of the oldest establishments in the wealthy section of town, it was known as a waterhole for the older, well-heeled generation. On any given night, the bar was packed with locals, mostly singles, seeking companionship and if they got lucky, a dinner date.

Securing a table, he ordered dinner for his family, pulled out the playlist, took the stage and began his first set. After the first song, there was a smattering of applause, clearly, those at the bar were more interested in finding love than paying attention to a crooner singing about love. With years of singing in casino lounges, he was used to the audience placing its interest elsewhere, that was part of the job. He was doing what he loved the most, singing and for that he was thankful. Forty minutes and ten songs later, he took a break and joined his family. Dolores was beaming with pride when Michael sat down. She showered him with love, doting on his every word. Michael Jr's reaction was, "Wow," the one expression that encompassed all his feelings. After two more sets, Michael gathered his family, paid the dinner tab and drove them home.

"There were a lot of pretty single women sitting at the bar," noticed Dolores. "Your last girlfriend didn't quite work out but you never know what's waiting for you."

"Thanks ma, I appreciate you looking out for me but I'm not ready for another steady girlfriend, think I'll play the field for a while. I'm happy, truly I am. After all, I have you and Michael Jr and that's more than I need."

"I don't want you to be lonely. You have suffered enough." She had promised herself never to bring up prison time and she was angry at herself, damn, it was all that wine that was talking. "I mean," she stuttered.

"Ma, I understand exactly what you are saying. As much as I want to and as hard as I try, I can never get back those twelve years. I stopped trying but I have not stopped trying to get my name redeemed and my accusations exonerated." They both shed tears as he pulled into the driveway, parked the car and walked silently into his home.

"Life ain't perfect. Right grandma. Look at me, I sure ain't perfect!" said Michael Jr.

"Whoever used the words ain't?" said Dolores.

Their scheduled vacation quickly came to an end. Michael returned his mom and son to the airport and they resumed their lives. He was forever grateful he had saved enough money to pay for their trip and for the beautiful memories they implanted into his heart. The love of a woman may come and go, but his love for his mother and son never skipped a beat, it was an unconditional love, one he could always trust and rely upon; it was literally until death due they part.

Placing the luggage at the ticket gate, they hugged and kissed good bye, "Until next year," said Dolores as she grabbed Michael Jr's arm and they walked toward the security gate.

Michael shed tears, he dearly loved his family and appreciated the love from his mother. She never once chastised him for his time in jail, nor brought up the fact she had raised his son, her grandchild. Dolores was a woman of strength, a woman so filled with altruistic love that nothing could shake her endless devotion to Michael, her spouse and daughter. A love everlasting a love of enduring through time. Her display of love was truly synonymous with the definition of ethereal.

Drying his eyes, Michael exited the airport and drove home slowly. Mulling over his mom's advice, he decided to pay the watering hole, where he often performed, a visit. It was his day off, he didn't have a gig and he didn't want to return home. Shuddering, suddenly he felt lonely. After a week of so much affection, he suddenly felt all alone. Making a left and a right, he drove north, exiting at Sahara.

Mid-week, no one was entertaining, yet the bar was teeming with singles, drinking the daily special. Coaxing himself, he took a seat at the bar and ordered the special. When the waiter set the drink in front of Michael, he added it was on the house, "The boss loves you. On the low down, whenever you sing, we do a lot more business. To tell you the truth, you have made a strong impression on the women. Those romantic songs seem to help them find love, at least for a night. For me, it means a few extra bucks while I keep adding to their bar tab. Keep on singing, Michael."

There were two women (Laura & Christine) sitting next to Michael at the bar. Laura said "That's a great suit! You remind me of the men in the neighborhood where I grew up. Very nice!" My girlfriend and I are meeting for dinner. Would you like to join us? Michael replied: "Only if you allow me to pay".

During the entertaining conversation, Michael mentioned "I love to cook, I have lived in Las Vegas for a long time and cooked at some great Italian restaurants. Look, I know we don't know each other, but how about the two of you come to my home and I promise, I will make you a meal you can only dream of. Both of you come. We are strangers, but after dinner at my house, we will be friends for life." Laura & Christine agreed to meet Michael for dinner.

On the way home, she and her friend discussed the invitation. They were a little reluctant going to a strange man's house for dinner. But they were assured other people would be there and it might be a nice way to meet new people.

They agreed it would probably be a lot of fun.

The next morning Michael drove to the grocery store purchasing all the ingredients for a perfect meal for three, he wanted to impress both ladies. As he plucked each item from the shelves, his feet seem to fly off the floor. It had been a while since he had entertained in his new townhome. Anxious to make a great impression, he pushed forward with confidence. He knew they would love his food, but the rest of him, he wasn't quite sure. *So much baggage, a guy recently sprung from prison, could the new woman deal with that part of his past? How would anyone want me again? I'm turning sixty, working two jobs, my hair disappeared, how would any woman accept me as I am? I want love, I want to love and to be loved but it seems like a tall order after what I have been through. I still have my health, my talent to entertain and to cook. Weighing the good with the bad, I hope this new lovely lady can see her way to balance the scale in my favor.*

The doorbell rang and Michael lunged to the front door to greet the women who immediately ogled over the lavish display of food, "I can't believe how much food you prepared," they said in unison, "This is enough for several meals!" That dinner was the beginning of a intense caring love relationship between Michael & Laura. Together almost 24 hours a day from then on, the couple discussed many times what the future would hold and decided to embark on a new adventure: My Mother's House Italian Restaurant located in Sun City.

It was his dream come true. A place where he could

prepare food born from his heritage and a stage to perform. Three nights a week he puts on a stellar show, singing throwback songs from the fifties, accompanied by a white baby grand piano, saxophone and drums. Wearing a smile, he was doing what he loved best and the city responded in kind. The bistro has been a huge successful venture.

Rat Pack era kept alive at My Mother's House

Micheal Leonetti serenades patrons Jan. 3 at My Mother's House, the restaurant he owns with his wife, Laura Rispoli. Below, Chad Michaels plays piano.

By Jan Hogan
View

Frank, Dean and Sammy would feel right at home here.

At My Mother's House, 9320 Sun City Blvd., chef Michael Leonetti serves up Italian staples paired with just the right vintage music.

"I wanted this to be like what Vegas was," said Leonetti, who owns the restaurant with his wife, Laura Rispoli. "Unfortunately, although there are wonderful restaurants in Las Vegas, they're just restaurants. I wanted to do something a little different, bring back the way Vegas was, where people can come in and dine and hear phenomenal music."

Pianist Chad Michaels performs solo Mondays and Tuesdays from 6-9 p.m. Wednesdays through Saturdays, he is joined by drummer Ryan Rose and bassist Kirk Kuykendall. Diners can expect the songs from the Rat Pack days: "I've Got You Under My Skin," "You Made Me Love You," "Misty," and "Fly Me to the Moon" among them.

"We take special requests," Michaels said. "(Leonetti is) around to make everybody feel welcome. People start singing along, clapping. Everybody gets involved. It just makes the night really special."

Michaels, who got his start in Detroit and comes from a family of musicians, heads the self-named trio. Kuykendall, who has been playing for 36 years, can also be heard in the high-roller area of Bellagio and Dispensary Lounge.

"I didn't even know Sun City Summerlin existed, but it's a good deal, a good set up," Kuykendall said.

Rose's father-in-law, a singer, was

Rat Pack

In the 1960s, the Rat Pack had five members: Frank Sinatra, Dean Martin, Sammy Davis Jr., Joey Bishop and Peter Lawford. They performed at the Copa Room at the Sands. The group didn't use the name Rat Pack to refer to themselves, preferring The Summit or The Clan. The Rat Pack Mascots included Marilyn Monroe, Angie Dickinson, Juliet Prowse and Shirley MacLaine.
Vol.ibvegas.com

Birdland" and went off script to skat for a bit. The diners applauded her enthusiastically.

Las Vegas resident Audrey Smith, a retired music teacher, brought her 4-year-old grandson, Ryan Koons. She appreciated being able to bring him somewhere with entertainment, she said.

"We came out on a little date tonight," Smith said. "How many places can you go to in Vegas that have live music anymore? It used to be what we were known for. Here, it's very accommodating, very homey. It's very old Vegas style, which I love."

Leonetti opened My Mother's House after a career as a lounge performer, beginning in 1972. He has worked at the Marina Hotel, Caesar's Palace and MGM Grand. He learned to cook alongside his mother, Dolores, and grandmother, Julie, both deceased. Just like they did, Lionetti serves food on oversized plates good for sharing.

He still has the wooden spoon his grandmother used to hit him with when he acted up as a child. It hangs on the wall along with pictures of, who else, the Rat Pack, as well as other notables from Las Vegas'

MICHAEL LEONETTI

Michael never forgot his friends, nor anyone who showed him compassion. It was mid-week and he had been chopping vegetables, cooking sauce and preparing pasta. He needed a break from the restaurant and decided to pick up a few items at Smith's. Exiting the restaurant he drove a couple of blocks, parked the car in a shopping center and strolled up to the deli counter. A big, freshly sliced ham sandwich slaughtered with mustard, was on his mind. Patiently waiting his turn, he looked at a fellow standing ahead of him and instantly remembered his face. It had been eight years since their paths had crossed, but he never forgot the kindness that man had shown him.

"Do you remember me?"

The man turned around and stared into Michael's face with no recollection.

He said "No" I don't.

Michael continued, "I remember you! I was in a holding cell in Family Court waiting to be called. It was lunchtime and the marshalls and other employees were enjoying lunch. You opened the cell and handed me a hotdog and some candy. To this day, I think about your kindness and generosity and the way you treated me. You know, like a real person—compassion and kindness were rare at that time in my life. Michael, Michael Leonetti."

He reached out and shook Steve's hand. "I guess I don't look familiar, but your face, well, that is a face I could never forget."

Michael was near tears thinking back to the holding cell at Family Court.

"I have a restaurant, right around the corner, please come and be my guest." Handing Steve a business card, he extracted a promise that one of the good guys would be a guest in his restaurant.

A couple of weeks later, Steve booked a reservation for a dozen family members. Michael welcomed his fleeting acquaintance and gave both he and his wife a delicious meal on the house. When the group of ten departed they were overwhelmed with the food, the fantastic music, but mostly Michael's warm inviting personality. He was genuine. Presently, Steve and his wife Connee are close friends with Michael & Laura.

To this day, he still keeps a watchful vigil on his last pleading with the Supreme Court, periodically checking the docket to see if any new order or response has been written. Nothing, at the writing of this book, has happened but Michael hasn't given up on the Courts exonerating his innocence. There would always be reminders of his past, he didn't have the power to erase the conspiracy. All he could ever hope for was a courageous attorney who would press the Courts into allowing the case to be reviewed. As long as he has breath in his lungs and a beating heart, he will fight his case. He will never ever give up. Never give up on his innocence, his passion for singing, he passion for cooking and his passion for loving.

Epilogue

The reason this book was written is because there are so many that are falsely accused. As you can see from current events, the corruption in the political arena is widespread. Accusing Judge Cavanaugh and so many others accused on hearsay evidence without due process is unspeakable. I'm a firm believer that corruption hates exposure and what you do in the dark is what you are about. If anyone believes there is no God, think again! He is the rewarder of those who diligently seek Him.

1) Joseph in the Bible was falsely accused of raping Potifer's wife. He received 12 years in prison. When released he became the Governor of Egypt.

2) In the story of Job in the Bible, Job loses everything and God gives him back double. Michael has been given triple back.

3) During the course of this case, 11 judges recused themselves. This fact shows how deep and true this deception was. Never in history has a case experienced 11 recusals.

4) The day Michael went to prison, the purported victim's parents emancipated her and made her leave their home. Her parents knew it was all a lie. They were afraid I would get out of jail and sue them. You must ask yourself, if my daughter experienced abuse in any way, would I make her leave her home?

5) Michael never had the opportunity to prove his innocence. This entire case was a conspiracy about covering up a false arrest and potential lawsuit against the Las Vegas Metropolitan Police.

6) When faced with threats of assassination in jail, the judge (Jackie Glass) did nothing. She was compelled under 18USC subsection 4 to uphold that law and she deliberately broke it to protect those who committed the crimes. I tried to get the bailiff's name who was on duty that day. He heard and was involved in the judge's non-action to protect Michael. A letter was sent back to me advising they did not know who the bailiff was. Another cover-up because there is a roster sheet for signing in and out on a daily basis by these court employees.

7) Nine circuit judge Trott in Cooper versus Dumbnick made a very profound statement :

"It is abiding truth that nothing can destroy a government more quickly than to follow its own laws or worse to disregard the charter of its own existence"

Laura and Mike Leonetti